SUPER
GRAB A PENCIL®
Pocket
FILL-INS

Visit www.pennydellpuzzles.com for more great puzzles

First Bristol Park Books edition published in 2015

Bristol Park Books
252 W. 38th Street
New York, NY 10018

Bristol Park Books is a registered trademark of Bristol Park Books, Inc.
Published by arrangement with Penny Publications LLC
ISBN: 978-0-88486-600-8
Printed in the United States of America

SUPER
GRAB A PENCIL®
Pocket
FILL-INS

RICHARD MANCHESTER

**BRISTOL
PARK
BOOKS**

HOW TO SOLVE

Fill-In puzzles are crosswords with a delightful difference—we give you all the answers! You solve the puzzle by filling in the diagram with answer words reading across and down as in a crossword puzzle.

The answer words are listed alphabetically according to their lengths. Across and Down words are mixed together. Cross off each word as you use it. When you fill in words in one direction, words in the other direction will automatically be filled in, so remember to cross them off as well.

Each puzzle diagram has one word filled in to help you get started.

PUZZLES

3 Letters

AFT
AMA
ARE
CAT
COT
DAY
DOC
EOS
ERE
ETC.
IRA
NOW
ODE
POD
PRO
ROO

TIL
TOR

4 Letters

AGON
ALAN
ALEC
ANEW
BOAR
ECOL.
ERIC
FEND
FLOE
GANG
IVAN
LARA
MALI
MIRO
OAHU
OGRE

ORLE
REED
SLAG
SMUG
STAR
TENN.
TORO
URAN
URGE
ZERO

5 Letters

ELIZA
LURID
O'HARA
STOOP
TYLER
WOVEN ✓

6 Letters

ADAGIO

FAIRER

NASSAU

PSEUDO

RANTED

SIERRA

7 Letters

BUFFALO

REWOUND

RINGING

TOSTADA

8 Letters

COATTAIL

OUTDATED

2

3 Letters

AAH

AIL

EEL

ENG.

HUN

IRS

MAE

NAB

NAE

OLE

RAN

SRO

TAU

TET

URI

USO

4 Letters

AGIO

CROP

EMIL

HA-HA

HOED

INTO

MYTH

NULL

OCHO ✓

TOPI

X-RAY

YETI

5 Letters

DACHA

DEBIT

DEEDS

EDSEL

LEADS

REACT

SNARE

TRAIT

6 Letters

AGOUTI

ANGORA

ANORAK

ATONAL

BONNIE

CARREL

CONSUL

8

CRATED	KLAXON	YELLED
ENOUGH	RETAIL	
HANGAR	ROBOTS	**7 Letters**
HEALED	SMITHY	ARRESTS
HECTOR	SMOOTH	HONESTY
HOOPLA	TEMPLE	

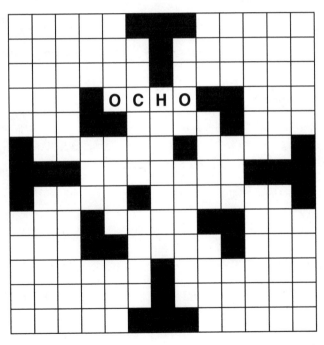

3

3 Letters

AGO

ALT.

APE

AWE

ERA

HAN

IDS

IRE

POE

RES

SEE

TSP.

4 Letters

ADEN

ALDA

ASEA

CELT

EARL

ERIE

GNAR

LEER

NYET

ODIN

OPEN

REAP

ROME

ROVE

RUSE

TEND

5 Letters

ARDEN

CASTE

ENATE

IDLER

INURE ✓

NESTS

PESTS

SITKA

6 Letters

AEGEAN

AGENDA

ASSENT

DEPORT

EDGIER

EERIER

ETUDES	NEARER	UPRISE
EVENED	RHODES	VEERED
GLORIA	SERAPE	
KEEPER	TAILOR	**7 Letters**
LAMENT	TELLER	WETLAND
LARVAE	TIRADE	YIELDED

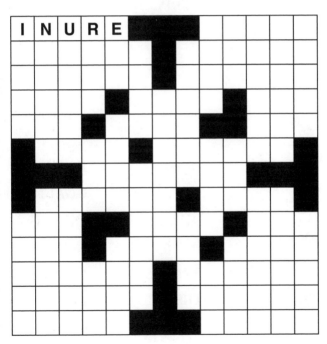

3 Letters

ADE

BEE

CEO

E'EN

EVE

HIT

ICE

I'VE

NIM

POI

SEA

SON

TEA

TNT

4 Letters

AGEE

AREA

CREE

DRAT

EDGE

ETRE

FRAT

GILD

HONE

MART

NERO

OLIO

OMAN

ONER

OPTS

PENN.

TEST

TORS

5 Letters

EGYPT

NEEDY

NEHRU ✓

OUNCE

PRINT

SCOPE

STAGE

6 Letters

CASHEW

EARTHY

EASING

GOALIE

INNING

INTACT

LATTER

LETTER

OBLIGE

PARIAH   TRENDY   **8 Letters**

PEALED   APIARIST

PENROD   **7 Letters**   ATTACHED

REESES   ECHELON

REFLEX   HOGWASH

SEXTET   MEDICAL

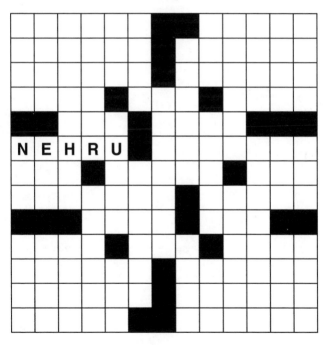

5

3 Letters

AND
BUT
EDO
EKE
GAR
GYM
IDA
ILL
KEG
KIN
LEI
MEL
O'ER
OIL
OOH
RHO
TAR

TIE
TOM
URN

4 Letters

ACHY
AIRE
ALGA
ANON
ARNE
ASHE
ATTU
BLAT
CHAR
ELLA
ERLE
EWER
HEEL
IONA
LORI
ORDO

OSLO
RODE
RYAN
SANE
SARI
SCAN
TANG
TGIF
TRON
VARY
WALL
WEAN

5 Letters

ABBES
ALLEN
AMISH
BITTY
CROFT
ENEMY

HAGAR

NOBLE

NOSED

OFTEN

TAFFY

THEME ✓

6 Letters

DOTING

EVELYN

7 Letters

NEEDFUL

OKINAWA

8 Letters

NORTHERN

ROSSETTI

3 Letters

EVA

INS

ION

IOU

KIP

LYE

MAP

MOE

NEE

ONE

RAF

RED

SIR

SUE

4 Letters

AVID

BOND

DART

EELY

LAND

LIEU

OISE

RACK ✓

RANT

RENT

VOTE

YSER

5 Letters

BRASH

HEMPS

LISLE

PERKY

PETER

SILKS

STEED

TESTS

TSKED

YESES

6 Letters

AIDING

ATOMIC

DELTAS

ELEVEN

ELOISE

ERASER

GREASE

INFORM	NOSIER	VIOLET
KETONE	ORNATE	YIELDS
LLAMAS	ROMANO	
LOATHE	SHRANK	**7 Letters**
NANTES	SLYEST	KOREANS
	TEMPER	NUREYEV

7

3 Letters

AKA
ALF
AXE
CPA
DAN
EDD
ESP
EST.
GOT ✓
IWW
LED
NED
RIO
ROE
SUB
THY
WAC

4 Letters

AHAB
AXIS
CASA
DYNE
ECOL.
ELSE
ENOW
HOWE
ICES
LEAH
LIDO
PALS
PARE
SWAM
TASK
YEWS

5 Letters

EAGLE
ETUDE
MOWER
SATED
THOSE
TOTED
VEERS

6 Letters

ABSENT
ACCEDE
ADORED
BASHED

COBWEB	IRONIC	UPDATE
DECKLE	KOALAS	WINGED
EDISON	LUNACY	
EFFETE	SCREEN	**8 Letters**
EGRETS	SLEEVE	ELECTRIC
FEEDER	TSETSE	LEOPARDS

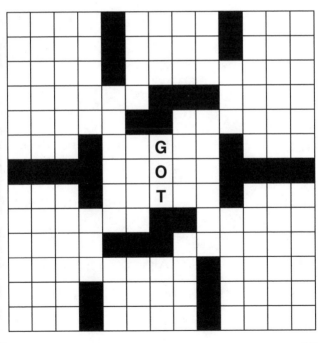

8

3 Letters

AMT.

AVA

CEE

ELI

ENS

ESS

GAL

GEM

LEN

LES

LON

MID

PAS

SEN

SGT.

SHH

4 Letters

DESK ✓

DINA

EVER

IDOL

LOPE

REND

VOID

YARE

5 Letters

ATTAR

ELEGY

LEADS

LETHE

NEGEV

ROOST

SEEDS

SPELL

6 Letters

ACUMEN

ASSURE

AVENGE

BEANIE

BIKINI

COULEE

DURING

ENESCO

ERRING

ICE AGE

INSECT	RANGER	TURTLE
INTERN	RESCUE	UNISON
LICHEN	ROVING	
NORMAL	SPONGE	**7 Letters**
OOLONG	TALONS	EARNING
RAMROD	TENSER	SOUNDED

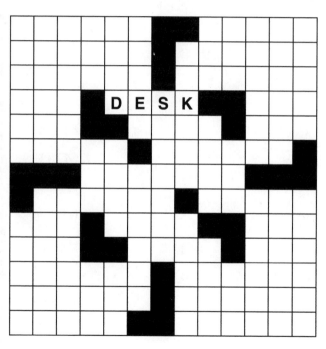

9

3 Letters

ANY
AVA
BID
ELD
EST.
HMO
LEI
MAE
MPH
OTO
POE
RIM
RNA
ROC
TIN

USN

4 Letters

ANIL
ANOA
ANTE
DROP
ECON.
ECRU
EDDY
EIRE
ETNA
GARB
GEER
OPEN
PIER
ROLE
ROTO
SEER

SPAS
ST. LO
TENT
UPON

5 Letters

ABACI
ANDRE
DANCE
DORIC ✓
ELSIE
GORME
IMAGE
NITER
ONION
OPTIC
ORLOP
UPSET

6 Letters	MENIAL	VESTED
AGENDA	NATION	
ARTERY	NIECES	**7 Letters**
ATONED	ORNERY	ESPOUSE
BRUTUS	PRIMED	GERMANE
INSIST	UTMOST	

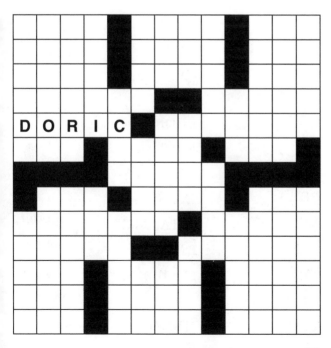

3 Letters

APO

EFT

ELF

FEY

MAC

NBA

NCO

OAT

OPE

OUI

PET

REM

SAN

THE

UNO

YEN

4 Letters

ABBA ✓

AFAR

ANTA

APED

BLUR

CONE

CORN

DEBS

DIET

DING

ECON.

ERST

ICON

INCH

IOTA

LATE

LYLE

MAYO

MEMO

NAST

NEAT

NO-NO

OGEE

OPEC

OTTO

RANI

RIOT

RSVP

SAVE

TOES

VAIL

VEEP

5 Letters

AARON

AUDIO

GNARL

SNORE

TATAR	FLEECE	**8 Letters**
TRAIT	NEEDLE	AWAITING
		BONA FIDE

6 Letters	**7 Letters**	EDENTATE
ALBEIT	COMPUTE	SUBPOENA
ANDREW	EPISODE	

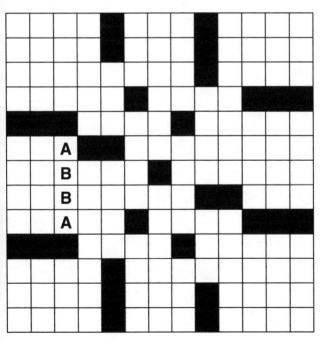

11

3 Letters

ABE
ANA
AND
APE
ASK
BEA
DUG
EEL
E'EN
ERA
LEE
LEI
LIE
NIM
NOD
ONO

PHI
RAY
ROD
USO

4 Letters

AXEL
DOUR
EDDY
ERIK
ERIN
ETRE
EXIT
EYRE
HONE
IONA
KENO
KIEV
NAME
RAKE

SEEK
SETH
TIER
TRAP
TRIG
TYRO
VEER
YOKE

5 Letters

ADLAI
ITALY
KRILL
LEVER
LIVER
LLOYD
OAKEN
PAY-TV ✓
REFER
RIANT

WELTY	STELLA	**8 Letters**
YEATS	TWELVE	ENTITIES
		GOOFBALL
6 Letters	**7 Letters**	UNSEALED
ALLEGE	BLANKET	VALHALLA
REVERE	LOYALTY	

12

3 Letters

AGE
ATE
CNN
DUE
EDO
ERE
HIT
LOT
MIG
NON
ODA
RED
RES
TLC

4 Letters

ANTI
DEAN
DREW
ELAN
ELLS
ERSE
EZIO
IDES
LILA
MELD
NOTE
OAST
ODOR
SODS
TEED
ZORI

5 Letters

CEDED
CROCE
ELIDE
ICIER
MONET
OMEGA
RADIO ✓
STAGE
WALDO
WRIST

6 Letters

ANTLER
ARENAS
DASHER
EDENIC
EMILIO
ENCODE
ENSURE

ENTIRE	RETIRE	LUCERNE
GERALD	SALTED	
GOLDEN	STATED	**8 Letters**
MOTELS		ITERATED
NATURE	**7 Letters**	NEWCOMER
RELATE	DESMOND	

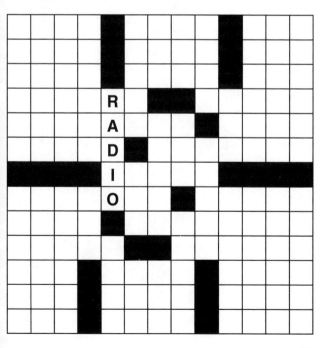

3 Letters

ADD
ARF
DEN
DOW
DRY
GAD
IRE
IRS
MET
MOI
ORO
REE
REF
SIS
SOP
TED

TNT
URI

4 Letters

ABUT
ATTU
AWED
BABS
BATT
COTE
CRUZ ✓
EAVE
ERLE
ESNE
ET AL.
KEEL
LAND
LEDA
MUDD

OLEO
OPAH
OTIS
PEAS
RULE
SCOT
SEMI
SLAT
SPUR
TOFU
TYKE
ULNA
VOLE

5 Letters

EXIST
MOGUL
PARCH
STAFF

6 Letters

ABOARD

ADJUST

BUFFER

FLORIN

IMPOST

IODIDE

OLDEST

ORATED

REALLY

ROBUST

STREAK

STUFFY

7 Letters

JUKEBOX

UTILIZE

14

3 Letters

ALL

ANY

DOE

DOR

EDD

EKE

ENS

GAL

LET

LTD.

MEL

ORE

PER

PSI

RTE.

SLY

STY

4 Letters

ASST.

DELE

DICE

DRAT

EDGE

EERY

EFTS

EVES

HATH

HEED

HOPI

LENO

OPAL

ORTS

PERE

PLOD ✓

SASH

STOA

TENT

UTAH

YAWL

YSER

5 Letters

GATOR

LEERY

MAPLE

MOOLA

OOZED

STEED

6 Letters

ALERTS

EMENDS

FREEZE	**7 Letters**	**8 Letters**
LINTEL	AUSTRIA	ALIENATE
LOLLED	LOW TIDE	EVIDENCE
OOLONG	PLOPPED	RECORDER
TALKED		TENNYSON
TERCET		

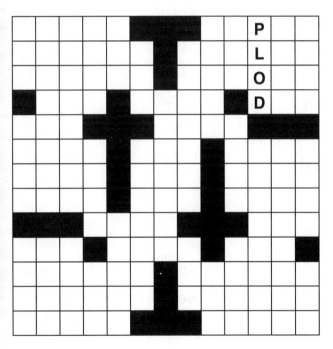

15

3 Letters

BOG

COY

EAR

ELL

LIP

ODD

OLE

POI

RBI

SOL

TAG

'TIS

ZEE

4 Letters

ANEW

ARCS

BULL

BUZZ

ECHO

ECOL.

EPEE

ERNE

ETNA

ISAR

LASS

LENA

MENU

MESS

NOEL

NOLA

ONCE

RHEA

RYES

SCAN ✓

ST. LO

TEND

5 Letters

BEEPS

EDITH

GLINT

HYDRO

SATYR

TABOO

6 Letters

ALBANY

ARNOLD

ASLEEP

ATONAL	SIEGED	ZENITH
AZALEA	SMILED	
BRAYED	TERCEL	**7 Letters**
LAMENT	TRIODE	LYRICAL
LAZILY	UPROAR	REENTRY
NICEST	YELLOW	SHELLAC

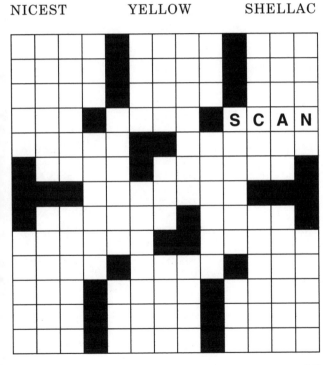

16

3 Letters

ARE

CEO

DYE

EMS

EMU

NIT

PAS

RAF

TAD

TOO

4 Letters

ALDO

BARI

CENT ✓

COMO

DOOR

EROS

ERRS

HYMN

IAGO

IRMA

ITER

NOSH

OMAN

SINE

STAT

STEW

STOL

TIDE

TOES

TOPS

VEEP

YAMS

5 Letters

ADOBE

BRIEF

CRAVE

EDICT

ISSUE

ORSON

PSALM

SINCE

TARDY

TENET

WAHOO

6 Letters

ADAGIO

ARARAT	OXFORD	YONDER
DEFAME	RANTED	
DRAPED	RASPED	**7 Letters**
DREAMY	REESES	EXTREME
HEALER	TEASER	LINSEED
OBLIGE	TIMING	TRODDEN

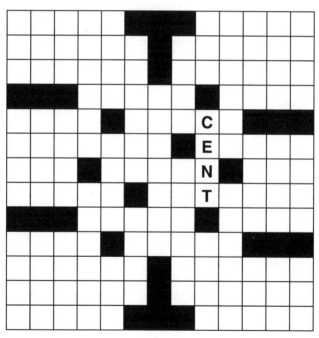

17

3 Letters

AVA
GNU
HAT
HUM
ILK
JAG
ODE
PTA
SEA
SON
TIC
TIE
TIM
VIM

4 Letters

ACHY
ANAT.
ASTI
AVAR
AVIS
CEIL
CURE
EURO ✓
GAME
HACK
ICON
INCA
JAVA
LAVA
NESS
NO-NO
ONER
ORAL
ORAN
PERU
RENO
SIZE
SLOP
SWAB
URAN
VASE
WARE
WISP

5 Letters

ADIEU
ENNUI
INNER
OOZES
REPAY
VYING

6 Letters	LEGUME	WAITED
ADROIT	LINERS	
DWIGHT	SACRED	**8 Letters**
ERMINE	SHOULD	BALUSTER
HERESY	SWEETS	MONSIEUR
HOT ROD	TEMPLE	

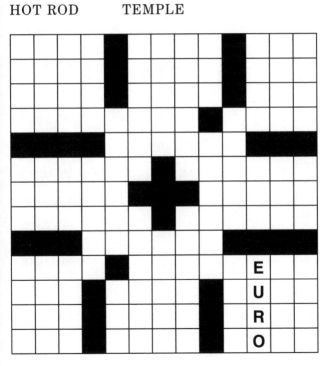

18

3 Letters

ALY

AMP

E'EN

ELI

GEE

GIL

HOB

IRA

LAY

NED

RAP

REM

RES

RIM

4 Letters

AERO

AGRA

ALAE

ANTA

APOD

ARIA

CITE

EBON

GLIB

HOPE

LIME ✓

NATO

NYPD

OBEY

RAMA

SEME

SNAG

SWAP

TAPE

TASS

WARP

YARN

5 Letters

AGLOW

AHEAD

AVISO

CONES

DEANS

ERICA

HAGAR

HARTE

LARRY

PEACE

SHAME

6 Letters

APIECE
ARABIA
BYLINE
EERIER
ENTREE

GEARED
JALOPY
NORMAN
OLIVER
PILOTS
REJECT

YAMMER

7 Letters

ESTRADA
RENEWAL
YEAR-END

19

3 Letters

AMA
AWL
BOA
EYE
MOI
NOW
NYE
ODA
OTT
SOW
SRO
SST
SUM
TIL
TNT
URN

4 Letters

ARNE
ASEA
ASHY
ATTY.
BLEW
CINE
DOWN
EGAD
ENID
FAWN
GILT
IN RE
ITCH
KANE
LEES
MISO
NOES
OBOE

ODOR
OGRE
ONYX
SANE
SO-SO
STEP
TRET
TYRO
VEAL
YO-YO

5 Letters

ANISE ✓
EXPEL
IONIA
IRONY
KAPOK
NYLON
RASPY
TOKYO

TONTO
YESES

TARTAN
VICUNA

PREFECT
ROMAINE

6 Letters

EMBRYO
ETUDES

7 Letters

ANTENNA
EROSION

8 Letters

MOTORMEN
POIGNANT

20

3 Letters

AGE

ART

CAD

CPA

ERE

GNP

INC.

IVY

MAE

OIL

REE

TAT

TEA ✓

44

4 Letters

ANTE

ASHE

CLAN

DANE

DEAR

DUSK

EDIE

ELKE

ESTE

MA'AM

OMAR

ONTO

PUTT

RARE

REAR

SAGS

SAND

SCOT

TAOS

VAIN

5 Letters

EAMES

HASTE

HOLED

KOREA

MATTE

NEPAL

PINTO

SNEER

YELPS

6 Letters

ALASKA

ATTAIN

CANADA	IDEATE	UNEASE
DEEMED	PASCAL	UNHOOK
DODDER	SCREAM	
ESCAPE	SHAKER	**7 Letters**
GARTER	STANCE	AGITATE
HANSOM	TSETSE	IMOGENE

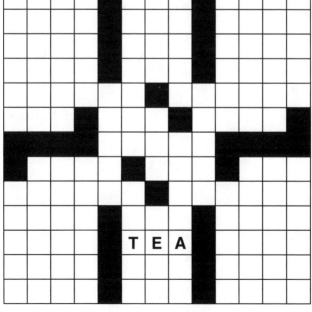

21

3 Letters

AKA

ALT. ✓

ARM

AVE.

BEN

CIA

ERA

ERR

IOU

LAD

LEO

OAF

ORE

REP

TKO

TUT

4 Letters

ALEF

EGAN

FLEA

GYMS

MYTH

OAHU

REAM

RHEA

ROLE

SILL

YARE

YODA

5 Letters

ACRES

EDGER

FACER

LOSER

OCTET

OSCAR

RISEN

STATE

6 Letters

AILING

ALKALI

AMANDA

CARROT

CASABA

CHALET

ELEVEN	ORIENT	TARTAR
EL PASO	RENTAL	TRYING
ENDURE	SHARKS	
LEASES	SLEDGE	**7 Letters**
LLAMAS	SOLIDS	HAGGLED
ORANGE	STRONG	TOGGERY

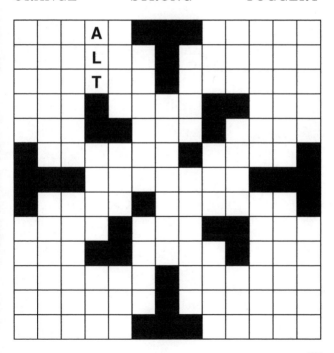

22

3 Letters

AMI

ANI

BON

DAG

EAR

EMU

EST.

HEW

NBA

NEE

NON

PAL

REO

USC

UTE

4 Letters

ACER

ADAM ✓

AMER.

ANOA

BASK

COME

DADE

EAVE

EDIT

ETRE

LAHR

LEON

MENU

NOSY

OGEE

PANE

RASP

TARN

5 Letters

ADDAX

CAMEO

ELAND

KEYED

LIONS

RHINE

RULED

TWERP

6 Letters

ACCORD

AGOUTI

ASHTON

AU PAIR	PESETA	TITLED
ITHACA	RECEDE	
KEEPER	REEVES	**7 Letters**
MANTIS	SESTET	ILL-BRED
ODESSA	SEXTET	PARASOL
OSIRIS	SKATED	RUSHING

23

3 Letters

ADS

CUR

EVA

FRA

HER

ICE

IRE

LET

ROO

SEN

TSP.

UNO

USA

4 Letters

AGIN

AGOG

ALEE

BERT

DEED

ELSE

EPIC ✓

ERNE

GENU

IBEX

LEAH

LENO

NOON

OUST

PAIR

ROUE

SAUL

SELL

SNIP

SOLE

SOUP

TENT

TOGO

URGE

5 Letters

ALONE

APRIL

FOUNT

HARPO

INDIA

LEHAR

NOTED

REPLY

SHELF

XENON

6 Letters

ADHERE

BOGGLE

CITRIC

DIONNE

ELINOR

ERRATA

GRAINY

ISAIAH

SALTED

SHAVER

SHRIFT

URSINE

7 Letters

ALCOHOL

IGNOBLE

STUNNER

24

3 Letters

ADE

AGO

ALY

MTV

OAR

O'ER

ONE

ONO

OPE

PAP

RIO

4 Letters

BLAH

DAVE

EDAM

GAGS

IBID.

IGOR

ITEM

LETS

LETT

LORE

NEST

NINE

RATE

TARO

5 Letters

BRIBE

EMILE

IRENE

METRO

MODES

MOSES

ORGAN ✓

TAMED

TORAH

6 Letters

ANIMAL

ARABIA

ARENAS

AROMAS

ATONAL

ATTIRE

DIESEL

HERESY

LAGUNA	**7 Letters**	**8 Letters**
MEREST	ESTRADA	ANEMONES
OMELET	GASOHOL	MILEPOST
PAGING	RISOTTO	TOOTSIES
POSING	TRIBUNE	TRAVERSE
RELIVE		

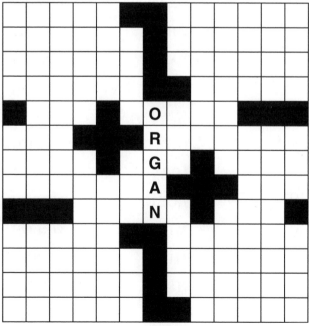

25

3 Letters

DOE

EGG

ELI

ENS

FAR

IRA

LTD.

MAR

OBI

ROB

RON

SAT

TAR

WEE

4 Letters

ACTS

ALOE

ARLO ✓

BATH

BERG

DANA

DRAW

EELY

ENOL

ERST

GNAT

ICKY

LULU

MILE

MINN.

NEON

NORA

NUDE

OLEO

OMEN

SYNC

TINT

5 Letters

AROMA

DATED

EPODE

GET IN

IMBUE

LOTUS

NEEDY

ORLOP

TIBET

VOWED

YAWED

6 Letters	FOREGO	SORBET
ABOUND	GERALD	
ADD-ONS	INDENT	**7 Letters**
ALLEGE	ITALIC	ACETONE
CORNEA	KRAMER	LENIENT
ENMESH	RELENT	VOLLEYS

26

3 Letters

ALE
ALI
ART
AXE
BOO
CAL.
DAW
DUO ✓
EBO
HOE
NED
NYE
SEE
TEA
UPI
URI

4 Letters

AERO
ALFA
ALOE
ANTA
ATTU
BRUT
CABS
D-DAY
DUKE
EASY
EBRO
EDNA
EELS
ENOW
EPEE
EYER
HERR
HOAR
IBEX
LADE

LEEK
LENA
LION
MASH
MOOR
NETS
NODE
OLIO
RAPT
RETS
RINK
SIFT
URAN
USED
WITS
YELP

5 Letters

EMEND
IBSEN

LINDA	AWAKEN	**8 Letters**
NADER	LATELY	OFFSHOOT
RATIO	OBEYED	RESANDED
ROSIE		

7 Letters

6 Letters   ALUMNAE

AROUSE   HOSIERY

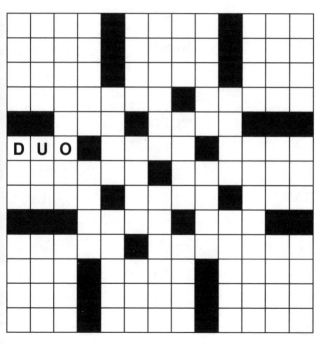

3 Letters

ANA
ANI
ELF
ERA
EST.
FOR
GAP
LOU
NAB
OTO
RAN
RBI
RON
ROO
SOD
SRO

4 Letters

ASEA
ASIA
CAFE
CATT
DAMP
DIME
EARL
EDAM
ELAM
EMUS
EURO
EYED
FEEL
IONA
KANE
LIFE
LOLA
LONI
MELT

NILE
NORA
ODOR
OLGA
ORLE
RAGE
RAMP
SANE
SEEP
SELF
SIGH
SPUN ✓
TARN
TIER
UGLY
YODA
YOKO

5 Letters

EELER

FROGS

LYDIA

NEEDY

SALEM

SHADE

TALLY

YO-YOS

6 Letters

EDISON

ORANGE

PARLOR

USEFUL

8 Letters

ARRAYING

DINOSAUR

28

3 Letters

AHA
ALL
ALP
BIG
DOT
EDO
ELI
EOS
GEM
GIN
HAG
LAG
LET
LOU
NCO
ODD
PLY
REX
SEE
SKI

4 Letters

ALOE
ARAM
AXLE
DEER
DIAL
EGGY
EMMY
ESNE
LACE
LADE
LANA
LAVE
LIND
LOSS
LYRE
MORN ✓
NEVE
NOSH
OLEO
OPEC
ORDO
TEEN

5 Letters

CURLY
EAGLE
ENEMY
GLOBE
LOLLY
OATER
PHONE
PYLON

6 Letters

AIRMEN

ARETHA

CAVEAT

EMERGE

EMPIRE

INHALE

IODINE

KOALAS

NUDGED

PLUMES

SECEDE

VESTAL

8 Letters

ALIENATE

SPANGLED

29

3 Letters

AGE
AGO
ASP
ATE
DEB
ETA
GAB
GAG
JAR
JAW
OAR
RAY
ROD ✓
TAD

4 Letters

ALAR
ARAB
ATOM
CAPT.
DALI
DEAN
EDEN
ELMO
ERIE
EWER
HALO
HAST
HOWL
IRAN
LAHR
LANE
LEAN
LIDO
LOWE
MOON
NAVE
OBOE
OKLA.
OKRA
OLAV
ORAN
ORCA
PLAT
POCO
REBA
RYAN
SIMP

5 Letters

APRIL
AROMA
EMMET
ERNIE
MOOLA

NORMA	**6 Letters**	WEAVER
OWLET	AMPERE	
SCOOT	ERRATA	**8 Letters**
TETRA	GENEVA	ARRANGED
TRIBE	PARDON	WEDGWOOD
	REARED	

30

3 Letters

APO

BEG

ERE

EVA

EVE

GIL

HEN

IRA

LOT

NAE

RIG

SAD

TET

TOR

4 Letters

ARIA

BEDS

DADS

EDDA

EKED

ERRS

FALA

FETE

FROM

JUTE

LAIC

LANI

LATE

PULL

REDS

REEL

TEEM

TUTU

5 Letters

GREAT

NACRE

PALER ✓

ROLES

TEAMS

TRICE

UTTER

6 Letters

AERATE

ALLOTS

CENTER

CRAGGY

DEFINE

ENACTS

GLIDER

JASPER

LEANED

LINAGE

ROMANO

STUDIO

TOURED

UPTAKE

URANIC

YONDER

7 Letters

AURICLE

CRADLED

HIPSTER

8 Letters

PARALLEL

PECTORAL

31

3 Letters

ABE

ARC

ASK

BAH

EMU

EWE

KAY

LAW

LYE

OUR

RAM

UKE

YEN

4 Letters

AVER

CHUG

DEEM

DULL

EDNA

EPOS

GAVE

HINT

LODI

MERE

NAPA

NODS

OGEE

PASS

PAUL

REPO

5 Letters

ADORE

ALARM

EDGAR

NEHRU

SALES

SALSA ✓

STEAM

SURER

6 Letters

APIARY

ASHRAM

ASTERN

DEALER

ENSUES

GARAGE

HEEDED

KEEPER	STEEVE		MACRAME	
MALAGA			SODA POP	
NEVADA	**7 Letters**			
PONGEE	AMERICA		**8 Letters**	
REDIAL	ARDUOUS		AIRDROME	
SEDANS	ASSURES		RACCOONS	

32

ZEE

3 Letters

AIL
ALE
ALI
ARE
BUD
CHI
EDD
EKE
FLO
MET
MOT
NAY
OBI
ONE
USA

4 Letters

ABEL
ABUT
ALEC
ANTS
ASAP
CELL
CINE
EARP
ELLE
ELSE
HAFT
KINE
LOTS
NEAL
NILE
OVER

PATH
RATS
SEED
SEMI
STEP
VIES

5 Letters

ADELA
CD-ROM ✓
CRAZE
DEICE
REACT
RERUN
SMASH
TULIP

6 Letters

ALLIED

ARTERY

BOCCIE

CANAAN

HEELED

IBERIA

IPECAC

MANILA

NEATLY

OLDEST

RELOAD

RHONDA

TEASES

UNHAND

7 Letters

LANYARD

OSTRICH

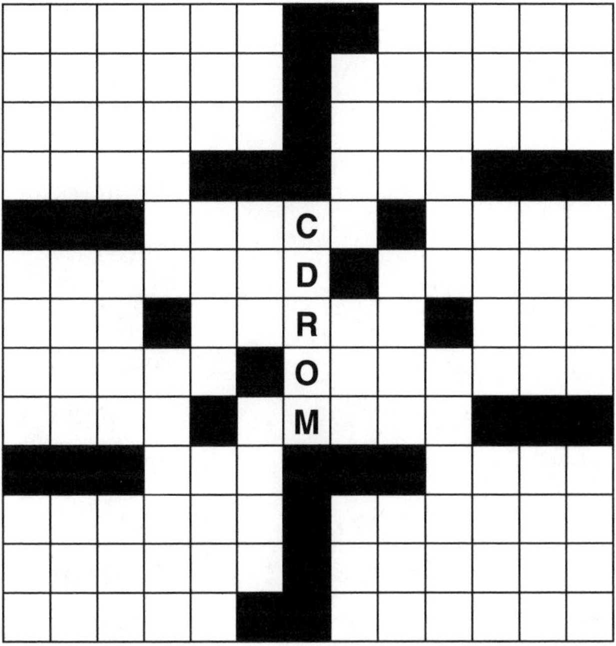

33

3 Letters

ASH
BEA
CNN
DAN
E'EN
ELL
ELM
ERA
KEG
LIE
LIT
LUG
MTV
NBC
NEO
UTE

4 Letters

AMEN
ANIL
ARNE
ARNO
CEOS
DONA
DOOR
EASY
ENOW
FEUD
FOPS
INGE
JARS
JOKE
LAOS
NERO
NONE
NOON
OISE
ONTO
ORAD
OTTO
PHEW
POSE
ROOD
SLED
SOON
UKES

5 Letters

AGILE
EROSE
ETHYL
GLORY ✓
LEGIT
LLANO
NITRO
OLSEN

OMAHA

VINYL

6 Letters

ADDLES

AVOWED

CAPOTE

MOLDED

7 Letters

DOWAGER

ENEMIES

LESSONS

RENEWAL

8 Letters

LEVERAGE

WEAKENED

34

3 Letters

BOW ✓
DEW
ELI
ENS
GAR
IDA
IKE
I'VE
LAB
LEN
MEL
NAG
ODE
ORO
PBS
TUT

4 Letters

AERO
AGNI
APED
ASPS
AWES
EPEE
ERNE
ERSE
GENU
IDOL
KEEN
NATO
NEAR
OLEO
PLOW
SEWS
SIZE
TASK
VEIL
WADI
WATT
WIMP

5 Letters

AGAPE
AGGIE
BERYL
EWING
GRIME
MOTTO
OWING
ROBOT

6 Letters

ADAGIO

ANGELS

BREEZE

ENAMEL

LOGGER

MAKERS

NAPKIN

NETTED

POTPIE

RAGTAG

RESALE

SODDEN

TWIGGY

WEAKEN

7 Letters

NANNIES

WINSLOW

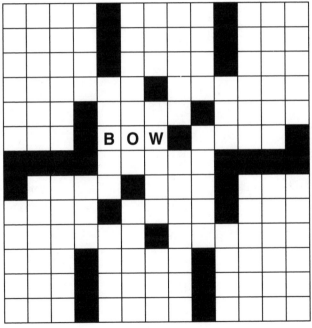

35

3 Letters

ABS
AGE
APE
BAH
BUR
EBO
EGG
EGO ✓
ETA
GEE
IRK
NOT
OPT
ORT
RAE
ROE

SEA
TEA
TIE
TOO

4 Letters

AMES
AREA
AVON
AXIS
BARI
BRIG
DENS
EBAN
ENDS
ENOW
EPEE
ERIN
GLEN

INGA
LIEN
MAXI
MINI
NAPE
NIGH
NINE
OMAR
OVEN
PALE
PALM
SEED
VIVA

5 Letters

ETAPE
GREBE
HOGAN
OATER

OKAPI

SMELT

6 Letters

ADHERE

EMBRYO

GRIPED

PAEANS

PARISH

PESETA

RAWEST

URGENT

7 Letters

ANOTHER

LARGEST

ROSTRUM

SUBSIDY

3 Letters

ACE
ALP
AND
CUR
EVE
GOT
INC.
LED
MOD
PUP
REE
REP
RIO
SAC
SIR
TAI

4 Letters

ACME
AWED
CHAD
CIAO
CUPS
DROP
ETRE
IN RE
KNEE
KNIT
LADE
LAPP
LOWE
OAHU
ONCE
PAIR
PERE
STAT

USED
VIVA

5 Letters

AARON
CELLO
DOWRY
ECOLE
ENOLA
IONIC
LATCH
LLAMA
LODGE
OILED ✓
OPTED
PHOTO
POISE
REVUE

RHONE	PARCEL	OCEANIC
SEDER	UNWISE	ORDERED

6 Letters	**7 Letters**	**8 Letters**
DEPICT	DENEUVE	LYRICIST
HOOVER	MARTINI	PRESIDIO

OILED

3 Letters

AGE
AHA
ATE
AWL
BLT
BUS
EDO
ERE
LAC
LAY
LID
LI'L
MAL
MEW
MUD
NAT
ORE

OWL
SEA
'TIS

4 Letters

ABBA
ACES
ACRE
ACTS
AHEM
ALAN
A LOT
ANKA
BROW
CULT
D-DAY
DELI
EDEN
ELLS
ESTE

EVAN
HANK
KIWI
LAKE
LATE
MEMO
ODOR
OLAV
OLIO
PEAL
RIGA
RUDE
URAL
VIOL ✓
WHET

5 Letters

ARBOR
CHAFF
EDITS

FARMS		DEFINE		RETAIN	
OINKS		EL TORO			
OSAKA		ERASED		**7 Letters**	
		HURRAH		ETERNAL	
6 Letters		LEVANT		HELIPAD	
ATTEND		METEOR			

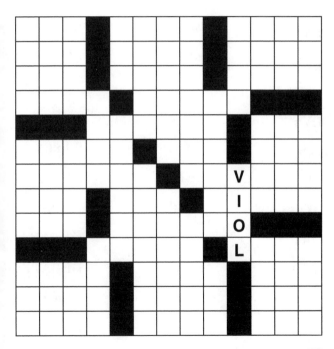

38

3 Letters

ALE

ALT.

BAR

DYE

ELD

EMU

EVA

ITS

LEE

NOG

ORT

RED

RET

SEN

80

TAR

WAC

4 Letters

CELL

DEWY ✓

EATS

EDDA

GALL

GNAW

GYRO

LENO

ONLY

RACY

RYAN

WADE

5 Letters

DREGS

DRESS

ERASE

GESTE

OSCAR

OWNER

SWARD

TRESS

6 Letters

ALUMNA

ATONAL

CANADA

DEBATE

ELATES

ERODED

GALORE	NOTATE	TENTED
GAMIER	ORATES	WHALER
INCOME	REMOTE	
NEATER	RIDDLE	**7 Letters**
NINETY	SHIVER	ERECTED
NITWIT	SIMILE	LARCENY

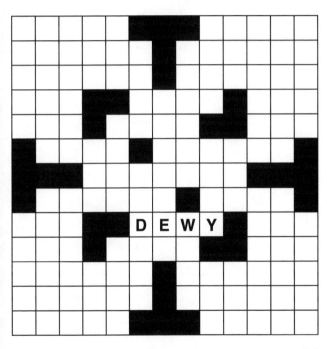

39

3 Letters

ADD

ARE

BEY

CIA

DAP

EBO

HIT

IRE

LAG

LIE

LYE

MAR

NIL

SOL

TAW

TOY

4 Letters

DRAM

IMAM

NANA

OISE

OREL

OWED

SARA

TROD

5 Letters

ADORN

BLAST

EARLE

LASSO

MILAN ✓

NEPAL

STONY

YEAST

6 Letters

ABATES

ABIDED

ALTARS

ANODES

DE SOTO

EDILES

ENESCO

ESCROW

HEALTH

HOGTIE

IBERIA

LENDER

LINEAR

LOWEST	STEREO	PATTERN
MALICE	TALLOW	
OYSTER	THRALL	**8 Letters**
PETULA		LANDLADY
RAWEST	**7 Letters**	NEEDIEST
SALUTE	ASHTRAY	

40

3 Letters

APT
BEN
CAT
EAU
EFT
EWE
FOE
HUH
INN
INS
IRA
IRK
LEA
MOI
NOR
OBI

OLD
REF
SEE
TAM

4 Letters

AGNI
AGON
AMID
ANTI
BOSS
CLAN
DEMO
EBON
EDOM
ENID
ERLE
HEMS
LYRE
MILA

NADA
NINA
ODIN
OLGA
ONES
PONE
RANI
RASH
ROLE
SCAN
SNAG
SORE

5 Letters

DEALT
SEVEN
SKEET
TEETH ✓
TORCH
TREAT

6 Letters

AFRAID

DORADO

LETTER

LLAMAS

MASTIC

SCARCE

7 Letters

ENSNARE

FISHERY

OMITTED

TWELFTH

8 Letters

SONATINA

VIOLENCE

41

3 Letters

ANT
ASP
BET
DIN
DUO
IRS
I'VE
NAN
RES
RNA
SOD
TAT

4 Letters

ADDS

AMOK
ANTA
DONA
ELAM
ET AL.
EVER
HONE
IDOL
INTO
LASH
LEDA
MA'AM
ORTS
POSE
SANS
SEEM
SPOT
SPRY
SUET

SUIT
TYKE
VAMP
YSER

5 Letters

AMIDE
ARMED
CHINA
DATED
HASTE
NESTS
SOCKO ✓
VIDEO
VOICE

6 Letters

ACROSS
ADONIS

BRIDAL	MONACO	**7 Letters**
ELEVEN	PISTON	AGELESS
ELMIRA	PLANED	MERCURY
ENRAGE	RESELL	OTHELLO
KEENAN	SHERPA	
MODEST	TASTED	

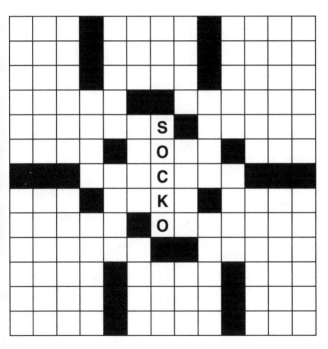

42

3 Letters

CHE
DOR
EEL
EGG
ELL
ESS
HEP
NEE
OAT
PGA
RTE.
SPY
SRO
TUB
USN

WOE

4 Letters

AVON
BERG
CASA
EBAN
ENDS
ERSE
HERA
HOAR
LEVI
NEIL
NOEL
NOON
ONER
ONTO
ORAN
ORES

POUR
RUSS ✓
SIRS
SLIP
SWAB
TINE
TYRE
WADI

5 Letters

AGATE
DIVAN
HEAVE
SPORE
YELLS

6 Letters

APPALL
ATHENA

GRETEL	REZONE	**7 Letters**
OPENER	SHOO-IN	CLEANER
PILATE	SNOOZE	ENLARGE
PLEASE	SWEARS	NURSING
POLLEN	THRACE	
RASHES	YOUTHS	

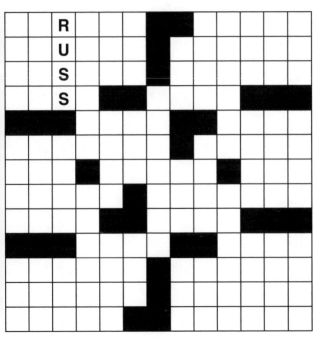

43

3 Letters

AIT

ALI

ALL

AMA

ARM

ETA

LAP

NIP

RHO

ROC

SIT

SKI

TEN

TOR

UFO

4 Letters

ACER

ANAT.

EAVE ✓

ECOL.

ELSA

ERAS

IRAQ

ITEM

LANA

LODI

NATO

NILE

ODOR

OMAR

OVER

RAMA

REDS

SARI

SIZE

THAI

VALE

WISH

5 Letters

DECOY

ELOPE

EMILY

EMMET

EQUAL

EVERY

KNOWN

KRILL

MELEE

PATIO

STEIN

SYRIA   ITHACA   ZEALOT

         KRAMER

6 Letters   RIPEST   **7 Letters**

AERATE   SALAMI   AUTOMAT

ENCINA   TRIVIA   TRAITOR

IMPALA   VIOLET   UNIFORM

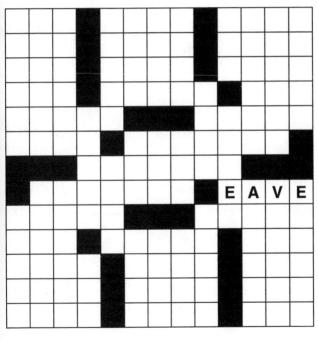

44

3 Letters

ACE
ADS
ALF
EDO
EVE
LEN
MOP
NCO
NEO
ONE
PER
RED
TAB
TOW
UPI

UTE

4 Letters

APSE
ATON
CHUG ✓
CODA
GORE
HAIG
IDLE
IFFY
IGOR
INGE
KARL
LEIF
NEON
OLEO
OSLO
PASS

POOL
SLED
STAB
STEP
TOTE
USMC

5 Letters

AERIE
CORNY
ILIAD
SCALD
SCENE
SPEAR

6 Letters

ALASKA
ASLEEP
AWEIGH

CREWED   OCCULT   TURTLE

DEWLAP   PEORIA

EILEEN   SECTOR   **8 Letters**

ICICLE   SLEEVE   LOATHING

MALONE   SNEERS   PANELING

MANTIS   SOONER

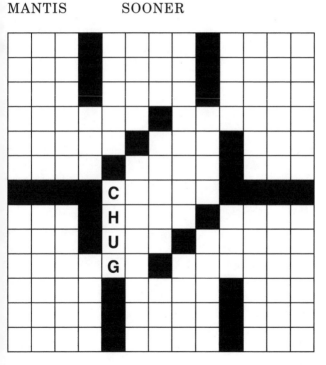

3 Letters

ADD

AKA

AVA

AVE.

CAD

CAP

E'EN

EKE

ENG.

GEE

GEM

MAE

NBC

SAD

SEA

TEA

TED

WEE

4 Letters

ACHE

ANNA

APIA ✓

DADE

DAVE

EASY

ERAL

EYER

GNAT

HERD

HOLD

IONA

LAST

LINE

LYES

NOUN

NUNS

OGEE

OGRE

OKLA.

POET

POSY

RELY

SEAM

SHEA

YEWS

5 Letters

BRADY

HARTE

RICER

SECCO

6 Letters	YELPED	DECK HAND
ASTRAY		GARDENIA
ENTREE	8 Letters	OPERETTA
HYMNAL	ACCENTED	REENTERS
NAMING	CAREENED	REVEREND
TEMPLE	CHEAPEST	

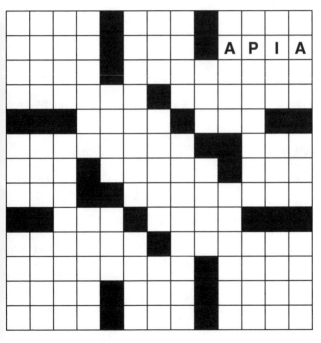

3 Letters

AMI
ASH
BIT
EBO
EMU
ERR
ESP
IRA
MIL
NAE
OWE
RAF
RAW
REM
RPM
TAI
TET

TOM
TSK
USO

4 Letters

AKIN
ALOE
AMID
ARAL
BAAL
DADO
EDEN
EMIL
ENOW
ERIK
ERIN
ESPY
EURO
FANG
FETE
ISLE

KIEV
LEER
LENA
LEON
LURE
MILA
NINE
PSST
REBA
RENO
RIDE
SITE
TINA
WORE
YOKE
YOKO

5 Letters

ALATE
AVISO
CRETE

DRUNK

LADLE

SEVEN

STENO

TAUNT ✓

6 Letters

GLANCE

VOLLEY

7 Letters

MADEIRA

NAIVETE

8 Letters

THANKFUL

TURNOVER

T A U N T

3 Letters

AGO
AID
ANN
ANT
CPA
DUO
EFT
EON
ERG
FUN
GOO
MOO
NOT
NUB
OOH
OTT

RBI
ROT
URN

4 Letters

AGIN
ALAR
AMAH
ANOA
BALI
BOND
CEOS
DIAS
DYER
ETCH
ETRE
GROG
NAPE
NODE
NOIR

OBEY
OTTO
PANS
PURR ✓
ROTE
ROTO
SURF
TARE
UNIT
YO-HO
YSER

5 Letters

ETUDE
LINEN
METAL
NINON
STEEP
TOQUE
WADED

6 Letters

CHATTY

EUCHRE

GROOVE

INDUCT

NOVENA

RAREFY

7 Letters

BABYLON

BUTCHER

8 Letters

HOMETOWN

NITROGEN

OPULENCE

QUANTITY

48

3 Letters

ALE

ANY

CUR

DAD

EWE

FDA

LAY

NED

NEE

OLE

ONO

OPE

SAL

SGT.

100

TSP.

4 Letters

AIDE

AREA

ASAP

ASPS

AWES

CREW

DEED

DOVE

DUEL

EDNA

FORE

INKY

MERV

ORCA

PEAR

PORT

SHAG ✓

TONE

WHOA

YELP

5 Letters

ACTOR

ELEMI

ILEUM

MEARA

ODDLY

PINOT

RETRO

RYDER

6 Letters

CANOLA

DAMSEL	PAPAYA	VULCAN
DEALER	PULLED	
DENOTE	REARED	**7 Letters**
DOLMAN	REPLAY	EARLDOM
IRONED	UNEVEN	JEALOUS
PANELS	UPKEEP	P.D. JAMES

S H A G

49

3 Letters

BOX

DAL

ERE

FLY

GOT

MOE

NUN

PAL

PRO

ROB

SIC

UNO

4 Letters

ADES

ADIT

ALIT

EAVE

EONS

ERIE

LETT

MAYA

POME

REAR

ROAD

SPRY

TEED

TORS

5 Letters

ADOBE ✓

ARENA

CHASM

DYERS

OARED

SLEDS

SPLIT

YODEL

6 Letters

ABOARD

ACORNS

CRUSTY

DELUDE

ELIXIR

ERASER

ESPRIT

HONCHO

IGNORE

IODINE	REFUSE	YELLED
LARGER	REPORT	
MIRAGE	SCAMPI	**7 Letters**
NODULE	TESTED	NOTEPAD
OPINES	THROAT	RECEIVE
POETRY	TROPIC	

50

3 Letters

AMA

APE

ATE

CEE

EBB

EDD

ICE

INS

IVY

LAB

LIE

LIP

LOB

LON

NIL

ORT

PEP

PTA

SOL

TIE

4 Letters

DEBT

WIRE

5 Letters

BARNS

EBONS

ELATE

EVERT ✓

EXERT

FATAL

FEAST

LIVED

STILT

TOWER

TWIST

XENON

6 Letters

ADROIT

ARLENE

DEEPEN

DIVINE

ECLAIR

EDITOR

EEYORE

ELINOR

EL PASO	RETIRE	WAPITI
ENRICO	SEASON	WARDEN
LASSES	TAPERS	
NOTION	TILLER	**7 Letters**
OMELET	TRAVEL	BALDWIN
REELED	VIOLIN	PEDDLED

51

3 Letters

AMP

ANA

AVA

AWE

BAA

BEE

GAL

JUG

LTD.

NOD

SHE

SIT

TBA

TED

'TIS

UPI

4 Letters

ALEE

AMEN

APEX

ARTY

BABY

BEEP

EPIC

EYED

GALA

GIDE

HIRE

IVAN

JUNK

KNEW

LETS

LYNX

MART

OAST

RAFT

RAGA

RIGA

SCAR

TIRE

TOLD

UPON

URAL

WWII

YOWL

5 Letters

ALOOF

ARIAS

BERET

HAIFA

LEMUR

LURAY   CIPHER   MELTED

REEDY   DEFAME   RECITE

WAHOO ✓   DEMURE   RELOAD

          EERIER   SLEEPY

6 Letters FEEBLE   STRAFE

ADESTE   MATHER

52

3 Letters

AIM
AMI
EDO
ELL
ERA
HAP
HER
LIT
MAC
MIN.
MOA
NBA
ONE
OUT
PAY
RYE

SRO
TIC
TOW
USS

4 Letters

AGHA
AHAB
ALAE
ALBA
AMAT
BAAL
BEST ✓
BOLT
BRAN
DHOW
EXPO
LAHR
LARK
NUTS

OAHU
OLGA
PLAY
RAMA
ROAM
SNAP
SODA
TABS
URNS
YUMA

5 Letters

AKRON
NEHRU
NICHE
SPODE

6 Letters

AGENDA
ANIMAL

EXHORT	**7 Letters**	**8 Letters**
INTERN	AUREATE	ATHLETIC
WALRUS	BEDOUIN	HENPECKS
WICKED	LASAGNA	KEELBOAT
	WINESAP	TEAKWOOD

53

3 Letters

BAT

BIB

CEO

CHE

DAL

E'EN

EKE

GAT

HOP

IRS

MAE

PER

RAN

RET

RTE.

SRO

TAI

TED

4 Letters

AFAR

BEST

DIET ✓

DREG

DUPE

PEST

PSST

REDS

RICE

VERT

5 Letters

EDGES

SEEDY

START

SYNOD

6 Letters

ABBESS

ADOBES

ASTERN

BEAGLE

BOOTIE

DEARTH

DRESSY

ELECTS

ERASES

ETCHED

FEALTY	SHEETS	**7 Letters**
GRACIE	SOBBED	DASHING
LEVANT	STREET	ENGORGE
LIMITS	TROIKA	OCTOBER
NETTED	UNLACE	RESOUND
ORDEAL	UPRISE	

54

3 Letters

ABC

AWE

EEK

ERE

ESS

FIR

FUR

GUN

IKE

IWW

LEA

NIX

REB

ROE

SGT.

SHE

4 Letters

ALAE

AMIE

ARAB

AREA ✓

ASAP

ASTA

BEAU

DARE

EARL

EARN

ECON.

ESAU

FEAR

FRAU

ITER

KEYS

KINE

LADE

LORI

PLUS

RAGE

WIFE

X-RAY

YETI

5 Letters

ANTES

ARGUE

AXIAL

FRAIL

O'NEAL

PIETA

READE

YEAST

6 Letters	GREASE	7 Letters
AGADIR	ORATED	BRITAIN
ARISEN	SOMALI	EXPLAIN
BOUNCE		FOLIAGE
CENSOR	WEIGHS	
FIESTA	WRASSE	UNSOUND

55

3 Letters

AHS

BAH

BET

BOA

DEY

DON

ERG

ERR

EWE

ILL

I'VE

LED

LOT

NED

ODA

PBS

RAE ✓

ROC

URN

VEG

4 Letters

ABBA

ABBE

ANNA

APED

ASHE

BRAE

BURL

EASY

EDOM

GANT

HARD

KATE

MEEK

OISE

RUDD

SHOO

SLAW

SPED

STEM

STET

ULNA

YORE

5 Letters

ANODE

BROAD

DREAD

DROLL

GET AT

GLADE

HIRED

SABIN   AMBLED   PANTED

TEETH   BOTHER   PRESTO

USURP   ELDEST   SCHEME

ENERGY   SLEEVE

6 Letters   ENTIRE   VIOLIN

AENEAS   MASHED

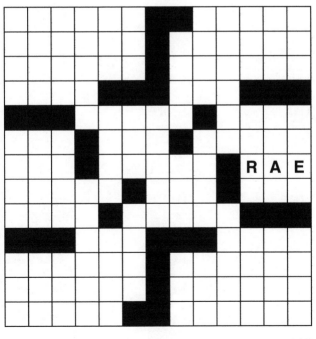

56

3 Letters

AIM

ALE

DEE

EOS ✓

GEE

HAT

IDA

NEE

NEO

NET

OOH

PFC

SUE

UFO

4 Letters

ARGO

ASTI

AVAR

ENDS

ERNE

GELT

HORA

LAVE

LOSE

NAES

NEAP

ORTS

RISE

ROSS

SKEW

VEEP

WEST

YELL

5 Letters

ASHER

AURAS

EASEL

ENATE

MEADE

RETRO

SLOSH

SNIPS

SPODE

6 Letters

ASLEEP

ELMIRA

EL TORO	LOOTED	**7 Letters**
ESTATE	NELSON	ECHIDNA
IRONER	SEATED	EMPTIED
KOREAN	STANDS	ERASING
LEARNS	UNSNAP	ITERATE
LESSEN	VIENNA	RESTYLE

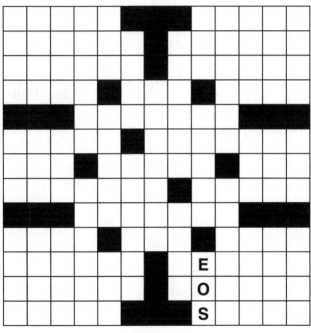

57

3 Letters

AVA

CBS

CHI

DOG

EAR

EBO

ELD

IRE

LYE

RCA

ROT

SEE

SOD

TUG

YET

4 Letters

BRIE

CLEO

COLT ✓

COSA

DUAL

ECRU

MAYO

MEND

ORAL

ORDO

RIOT

ROBE

STAG

STAR

TANG

TILT

5 Letters

ADEPT

CHOPS

DUELS

ELTON

FOLKS

LITER

ORGAN

RETIA

RUMOR

SAMOS

6 Letters

AURORA

BALBOA

DAHLIA

DIVERT

ESCORT

ICARUS	TEFLON	FAVORED
ORIELS	UGANDA	GLEEFUL
ORNERY	VASSAL	RESHAPE
SIGNED		SECULAR
SYRUPY	**7 Letters**	
TALKED	CRULLER	

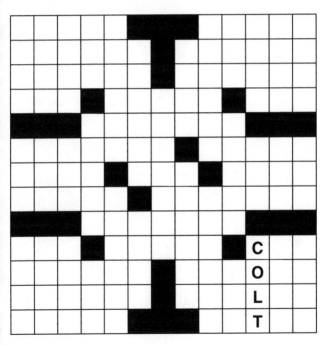

58

3 Letters

AGE

AIL

BAD

CUE

ELI

EMU

EVA

LAB

MAD

MAL

MAT

OPE

ORB

REE

4 Letters

AGAR

AHEM

DRAT

ERSE

FETA

GALL

HAIG

ICON

MILD

NAVY

PROD

RAYS

RITE

SPEW

WANE

YELP

5 Letters

ABASH

AMINO

ASNER

CREDO

CROCE

EDDIE

EDGED ✓

ENTRY

EPSOM

LLOYD

NANCY

PUREE

STEEL

TYPED

6 Letters

AERATE

APIECE	NAMING	**7 Letters**
CLEAVE	NUTRIA	ANEMONE
ELDERS	TREBLE	CRAMPED
FIANCE	TRYING	REBUILD
GLANCE	VELLUM	SCRAPED
HESTER		

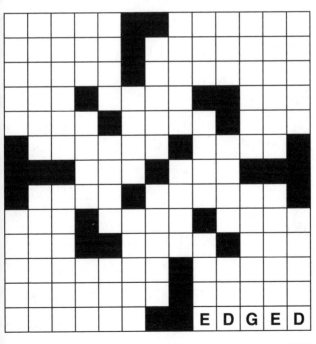

EDGED

121

59

3 Letters

ASP

EDD

FOR

GOB

ILK

INC.

NAE

SEN

SPY

SST

UPI

VCR

YEW

4 Letters

ANTI

AURA

BORE

CERE

DADO

DICE

DOME

EERY

ELIA

ERIC

ET AL.

ETNA

ICED

ONER

SEAN

SKEP

SPIN ✓

TADS

5 Letters

ASCOT

BELIE

EASED

OLEIN

TEENY

WELLS

YAHOO

6 Letters

ABATED

ATONED

BEREFT

CRATER

DARTED

DEBATE

DELTAS

MITTEN

OLEATE

REMEDY

SHEENA

SOARED

TONERS

VENICE

8 Letters

ANNOTATE

ENAMORED

LITERATI

PINNACLE

RESTRAIN

RINGLETS

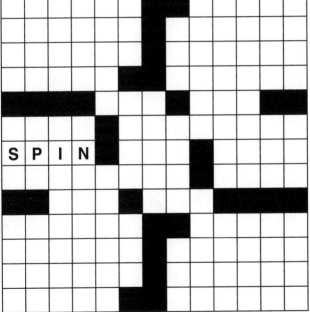

3 Letters

AND

ARE

CEO

ESS

MEL

NOD

ODE

ORT

OUR

ROM

SRO

TAD

TOO

TSK

WIN

4 Letters

AMAT

APES

BERG

BEYS

COMO

EDDY

ETUI

GOSH

INGA

INGE

LUAU

NEST ✓

OUTS

PINE

RAVE

ROTC

SHIN

STAB

THOR

TIDY

5 Letters

ERROR

EXURB

IRKED

LEMON

MEDEA

NICER

NOTED

RERAN

SWINE

6 Letters

CREDIT

HAULED

HOMERS

IMAGES

OLDEST

ORANGE

RATING

REEVES

SCARCE

SCRAPE

TERCEL

TUXEDO

7 Letters

ORDERED

OSTRICH

REGENCY

SPECTER

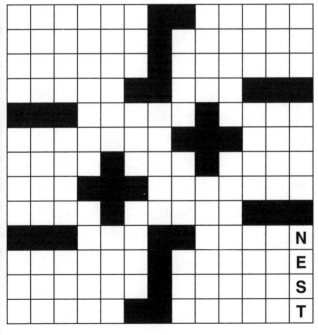

3 Letters

ABC

AHA

AIR

ATM

BEN

ETA

FCC

LAM

O'ER

OLD

ORO

PEA

RTE.

RUE

SIS

URN

4 Letters

AKIN

AMMO

ARTY

CASH

CHIC

CLAP

DEAN

DEBT

ELSE

EMMA

ERAL

ETRE

FAST

HARP

HOOD

IDLE

INCA

LEAR

LENA

LIEU

LOAM ✓

LUTE

MANO

MASK

MAYA

NAYS

NENE

NOME

NOTE

ONCE

OREL

RATE

ROOF

ROTE

SNIT

SPUN

SYNC

T-BAR

USED

YARE

5 Letters

CREPT

DUTCH

LENIN

LLANO

NEEDY

OTHER

OUTDO

TORTE

6 Letters

AFLOAT

ANTHEM

INDENT

PAEANS

3 Letters

ABE

AHS

DAP

GYM

MBA

NAG

NBA

NYE

PEG

RIB

SAN

SEA

TAT

THE

TIE

TIL

TSP.

YEN

4 Letters

ALAN

ASPS

BEDE

BIRD

BODE

DEMS.

EDOM

EIRE

FIAT

IBID.

IDOL

ISAR

I SEE

ITEM

KILT

LADS

NEAP

NOGS

RANK

REBA

RHEA

SHOO

SNAP

STEM

TARA

TEES

TERM

TREK

TRET

YODA

5 Letters

ARNIE

BRISK

FRISK

TIMES ✓

6 Letters

ADAGIO

DRIEST

KIBITZ

RIYADH

STAMEN

TIGHTS

8 Letters

AMETHYST

FREEHAND

FRENZIED

LEBANESE

NEEDIEST

SASSIEST

63

3 Letters

AAH ✓

AIM

AWN

CAP

DAD

DOR

ERA

HOT

ILL

IOU

ITS

NEE

NUN

TED

USN

4 Letters

ACER

AGIN

AIDA

ANTE

BEET

CUES

HAND

HEDY

INCH

MIDI

NERO

NINE

NYET

ODDS

PALE

PLAT

TRUE

WOOD

5 Letters

ELUDE

EMERY

GET ON

INPUT

LADEN

LITHE

NEVIL

TONGA

6 Letters

AKIMBO

CRANNY

EDITED

EILEEN	SNEERS	DEMEANS
KEENAN	UGANDA	LATERAL
MELDED	YONDER	LENIENT
NELSON		NOMINEE
NUANCE	**7 Letters**	NUREYEV
RELIED	ARMORED	TEL AVIV

64

3 Letters

ALT.
AWE
BYE
ELY
EOS
EWE
ION
IRK
I'VE
LEW
OIL
OWL
REO ✓
SOL
TLC
URI

UTE
VEE
VIE
YET

4 Letters

ADDS
AGIO
ALSO
DORA
DREG
EDNA
ELSA
EONS
HERA
HULL
IGOR
MAYO
MIST
PROP

PULL
RUST
SIKA
SLAW
SPAR
SPAS
STAT
TROT
URDU
YOKO

5 Letters

BEING
BLURB
CIGAR
HONEY
LIKES
SATYR
SHELF
SUITE

6 Letters

APHIDS

ISSUES

ORATOR

OYSTER

TALLOW

TOOTHY

7 Letters

ALIGHTS

CRUELTY

ELUSIVE

HUBBARD

LECTERN

OURSELF

65

3 Letters

AGE

AGO

AMA

AVE.

BLT

DOM

EDO

GOP

IRS

OBI

ONO

ROT

ROW

TAN

UNO

4 Letters

ADAR

AGNI

ERRS

GELS

ISN'T

LAWN

LIEN

LOBS

NICE

ORCA

ORDO

OVAL ✓

SHEA

SMOG

SOLD

VEER

5 Letters

AISLE

HAREM

HEAVE

HORDE

ISLAM

LEAPT

PASSE

TIARA

TORSO

TWIST

6 Letters

ACCORD

DONALD

ELUDER

HERMIT

IRONER

LEDGER STATED ESSENCE

MESHED T-SHIRT PETUNIA

MINDED VIRGIL RUN OVER

NEWEST VIOLATE

OCELOT **7 Letters**

SHAVES BROADEN

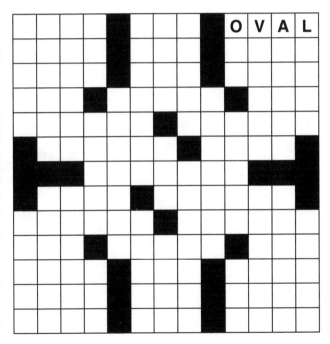

66

3 Letters

ANN

ATE

CEO

EBO

GEE

HEP

MIG

NED

NET

ONE

PGA

RES

RPM

SHH

4 Letters

ABEL

AREA

AVER

DART

EDEN

ERAS ✓

ERGO

GENT

INGE

IN RE

KANE

KARL

LEES

NEIL

OGEE

PINE

TOGS

VEAL

5 Letters

EOSIN

EWERS

HOMER

LLOYD

NONCE

O'HARA

PLIED

6 Letters

AGADIR

AGENDA

BERING

EAGLES

EERILY

ESPIED

IBERIA	REINER	INCENSE
KOKOMO	RENEGE	INTERIM
LENGTH		OREGANO
MODELS	**7 Letters**	SCRAWNY
ODESSA	ELYSIAN	SEALANT
RANGER	ESTATES	

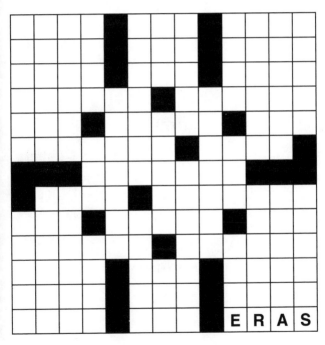

67

3 Letters

EKE

ERR

FBI

IMP

LET

MOB

NIP

NOR

ODD

PAR

RAD

SEN

SPA

TAI

4 Letters

ADAM

AGAR

ALEC

APIA

ARAB

AVOW

DEMO

DRYS

ELLA ✓

JUDY

LANI

LEON

NENE

OWES

SOPH

STAR

ULNA

YARD

5 Letters

BORED

EGRET

ERODE

GESTE

OTTER

PRIED

STAND

6 Letters

AMANDA

DIADEM

EDENIC

ERMINE

JASPER

MALONE

NEEDLE	TRIODE	ISOTONE
ONIONY	UPTAKE	LEASHED
ORDEAL		OPEN AIR
PADDLE	**7 Letters**	REMNANT
REGION	EPITOME	REUNITE
SERVER	INFERNO	

68

3 Letters

BAA
BOG
BUG
CAN
CEE
CNN
DOC
EEK
EEL
EVE
GNU
IAN
NBC
NCO
ORO ✓
PEN

PEP
REV
SRO
URN

4 Letters

APSE
AURA
BASE
DEAR
ELAM
ELLE
ERAL
EROS
I SEE
ISLE
KIDD
KIEL
LEER
LORI

LUCE
MOPE
OLAV
RATS
ROAM
SCOT
SLOE
TESS
TOLL
URAL

5 Letters

CYNIC
DONEE
EPODE
GOUDA
IRONY
LEROY
O'NEAL
YEAST

6 Letters

ARRIVE

DEMOTE

DORMER

EMBRYO

FEELER

STURDY

7 Letters

NORFOLK

ORDERLY

RECYCLE

SPEEDER

TOPIARY

YODELED

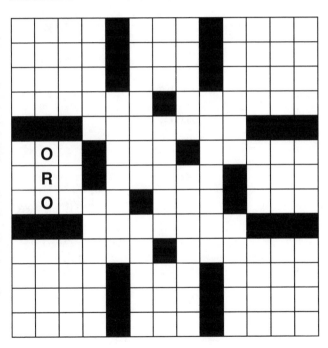

69

3 Letters

ACT

ART

BIN

CPA

CUR ✓

ELL

ENG.

ICE

IDA

INC.

KID

LAB

LAC

LAS

LEG

MAE

MED.

ROD

SEA

TNT

4 Letters

EARS

EDIE

ETRE

HOCK

HUES

KNIT

RUTH

SATE

SPEC

USSR

5 Letters

CLASH

GLASS

NICER

SABLE

SCOTT

SEEDS

SNEAD

STAKE

6 Letters

AILING

ALIBIS

ARCTIC

BISTRO

BRIDGE	KINDER	RAMADA
CARLIN	MELDED	SITCOM
CLAIMS	OCTANE	SLACKS
ESTHER	OLEATE	SPARTA
GEARED	ORATES	STANCE
HALTER	PASCAL	TIRADE

70

3 Letters

ALB

ANY

APE

APO

ARM

CAR

ELK

ESS

ETA

GEL

LED

NIT

OLD

PEA

RAP ✓

TSP.

UTE

VAT

WAD

YON

4 Letters

AMEN

ARID

AVON

BARI

BARS

BUMP

EDDA

GHAT

GOBI

INCH

NOSE

NOSH

OARS

OPEC

ORES

REBA

RODE

SELF

THEE

TO-DO

YARE

YARN

5 Letters

AWAKE

AYRES

ENVOY

FACET

HAUNT

HOARD

MEDEA

MINOR	ATTIRE	PASTOR
NEEDY	AVENUE	ROBOTS
STINT	DEEPEN	SNARES
	EL TORO	TIARAS
6 Letters	IMPALA	YIPPEE
ABIDED	ORIGIN	

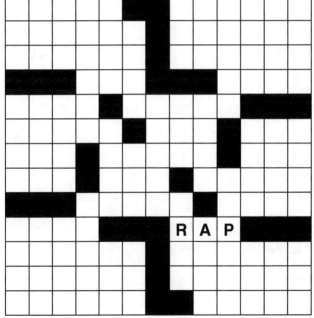

71

3 Letters

AAH

ANA

ENS

ERE

EST.

EVA

PBS

PRO

ROE

TEA

4 Letters

AGEE

ALEE

ASTI

AVAR

BRED

CAGE

DACE

DEER ✓

EATS

EDGE

ELIA

EYED

GENE

ICED

MALI

MEND

SNAG

TEEN

VERB

VIED

5 Letters

APPLY

EASEL

ESSEN

IVORY

RAGED

SEPAL

SLYLY

SPLIT

WILDE

6 Letters

AMPERE

BARREL

CITRIC

EDWARD

ELAINE

LLAMAS

MADCAP	PRATES	**7 Letters**
NECTAR	REMEDY	EMPEROR
ORANGE	RESEED	PERSONA
PAPACY	SHODDY	PRESSED
PARSON		SMILING
PLATES		VACCINE

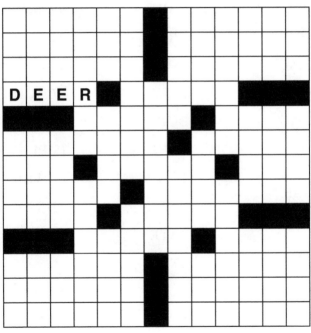

72

3 Letters

AIR

BAD

EDO

GOB

MAC

NAT

NEE

ORE

PAP

PSI

TOR

UPI

USO

4 Letters

ABBR.

ABUT

ARIL

ASEA

BLIP

CAPA

CRAW

EDIT

ELBA

EURO

EYER

GLOP

HYPE

LATE

LENO

LUKE

MALL

RAGA

RAPT

RENT ✓

SALE

SARA

5 Letters

ALAMO

AUNTS

COACH

ERUPT

IMPEL

RAWER

THREE

TIARA

6 Letters

ASTRAY

BERATE	MUSCLE	**7 Letters**
CURATE	ROTARY	PRIMATE
EMOTED	TOLEDO	RETREAT
ENCORE	UNITED	STRATUM
ISAIAH	USURPS	TRUSTEE
KEATON		UPSURGE

73

3 Letters

ADE

DOM

DON

EAR

EKE

EWE

LIP

MIL

MRS.

ORT

POP

REC.

RET

RYA

TEN

4 Letters

AMAT

APOD

BLAT

CEDE

EARL

EDGY

ENOW

EPIC

GAPE ✓

IRON

LAHR

LAMB

LEES

MAMA

MIME

OBEY

OGEE

PEWS

RUBY

TING

5 Letters

ERATO

OUSTS

PRESS

REPAY

RIGEL

YAWLS

6 Letters

ALBEIT

ANGELS

ANYHOW

ATTUNE

CURARE

DABBLE

GEORGE   POETIC   CATERER

GLIDER   RAIDER   ESCAPED

          URGENT   MUSICAL
LEARNS
                    QUARTET
OAKLEY   **7 Letters**

PEEWEE   BAROQUE

74

3 Letters

EVE
IKE
I'VE
LI'L
ODA
OWS
POT
RAG
RED
RES
SOL
TAR
TAW
WOK

4 Letters

ADES
ALDO
APIA
AWES
BONN
CASE
CROC
GEES
GNAW
METE
NAPE
ORAN
OWNS
RUHR
STEP
YOGA

5 Letters

ANODE
BASES
COAST
EELER
GESSO
MIAMI
NEEDS
STEAM ✓
STOWE

6 Letters

ALCOVE
AURORA
DONATE
EARNED
EEYORE

6 Letters		**7 Letters**
EILEEN	ORNATE	ANNOYED
ERNEST	SHAVES	EMINENT
INNATE	STIGMA	LICENSE
NIELLO	TANNED	OPINION
NOTION	TROWEL	YODELED
OPTION		

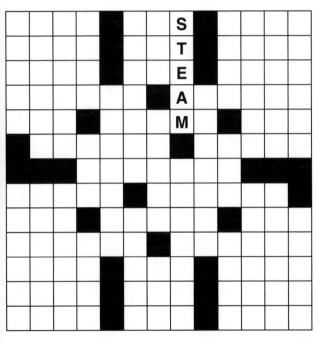

75

3 Letters

AIM

ASP

EDD

EFT

ETC.

FRO

LEE

OLE ✓

PAT

RYE

SOY

VAN

YIP

4 Letters

ALAN

ARAS

ARNO

BLAH

COLT

ELKE

ELSA

ENDS

GAVE

IDES

LAKE

LAWN

MANS

SCUD

SEER

SELL

SLIP

SOAP

TINT

TYRE

URAL

USES

5 Letters

ABELE

AESOP

ASIAN

BANTU

BATIK

DONOR

OMENS

TACIT

6 Letters

CRANES

EMBODY	RIYADH	**7 Letters**
FARINA	SALINA	CALIPER
FULLER	SLATED	GUMDROP
LANCED	TSETSE	INROADS
LITMUS	UNWRAP	LIKABLE
NEARER		TOPICAL

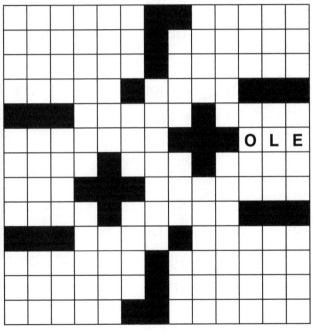

76

3 Letters

ACE

ACT

AVA

DOR

EYE

ICE

INC.

LAW

LEA ✓

MOM

NIL

PAS

SPA

TAO

USA

VEE

4 Letters

AGRA

BASK

EARN

GERE

GONG

HORA

OPAL

OVID

RAGS

RITA

ROTA

SCAB

SHEA

SLUR

STUD

TREK

UCLA

YSER

5 Letters

GORES

ROOTS

SEDER

SENOR

VIOLA

6 Letters

ARROYO

ATTIRE

BANNER

COAXED

COUGAR

EMERGE	OPINES	ECOLOGY
ENAMOR	PUEBLO	GLAMOUR
IMPART	RELATE	LECTURE
KLAXON		ORDINAL
LOAVES	**7 Letters**	PIVOTAL
NATANT	AWAKENS	RIPOSTE

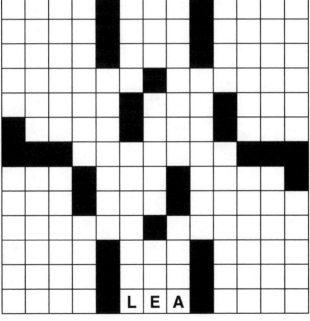

77

3 Letters

ANI

ARE

ATE

BOA

E'EN ✓

EON

INS

LAC

LIT

MBA

OAR

PAM

RAE

UNO

4 Letters

ACID

AGAR

ALTO

ANON

AREA

ARMS

CIAO

EBAN

ENOL

FATE

GARS

LIMO

NANA

NINA

PAGE

REPS

ROSS

SPCA

5 Letters

DENSE

HOMER

LADLE

MOTEL

OSAGE

OSCAR

PELEE

SEDAN

THERE

6 Letters

ABIDED

DELETE

EDILES	NIACIN	**7 Letters**
ENCINO	PREAMP	AVENGER
ERRING	SATIRE	ELEVATE
GAMINE	SERENE	GERMANE
LARIAT	STEREO	PULSATE
MENACE	TRENTE	REFEREE

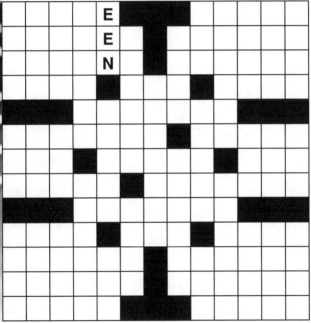

78

3 Letters

ABS

ADD

ART

AUK

DEN

EAU

E'EN ✓

PIN

PSI

RON

YAK

4 Letters

ARAL

ETRE

FLOE

GENE

OBOE

REEK

ROPE

SASS

SECT

SHOW

SNAP

TARA

TATS

WRAP

5 Letters

DIDST

EDICT

ENATE

FRIES

KEYED

KNEES

PER SE

STALE

6 Letters

ARBORS

BALBOA

HAROLD

LENDER

NIELLO

OFFICE

ORACLE

RACKET

SATEEN

COOPS	BLONDIE	**8 Letters**
FRANCE	DEBUSSY	INFERNAL
WALK-ON	ERECTED	REFRAINS
	ISLANDS	STRAINER
Letters	PADLOCK	TROUNCES
BATISTE	YAWNING	

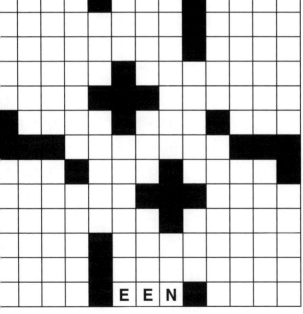

79

3 Letters

ANI
ASH
BAD
DON
DOR
ETA
HAN
HUE
IDA
IOU
OAT
ODA
OTO
ROM
SOL
SON

TBA
WAN

4 Letters

ABET
ADAM
ALSO
ANIL
ANOA
ASST.
AVES
BANS
DENS ✓
EDEN
HA-HA
HINT
JADE
LAVA
LEVI
LUAU

MAST
MITT
OUSE
OVEN
PLAN
POMP

5 Letters

ALAMO
DIODE
EARLE
ERATO
OMITS
RHINE
ROMAN
TWERP

6 Letters

ADDLEI
ALMOST

HAIRDO

NETTED

ODD-JOB

PUTTER

7 Letters

EXPOSED

LINSEED

MOTORED

RAT-A-TAT

8 Letters

DEBONAIR

EDITIONS

EXERTION

TEETERED

				■					■			
				■					■			
				■					■			
						■						
■	■										■	■
					■				■			
			■						■			
							■					
■										■	■	■
						■						
				■					■			
				■					■			
				■					■	D	E	N	S

80

3 Letters

DOG

EAR ✓

EFT

EKE

ELD

EST.

FAX

FLO

INN

LEO

MOO

OAR

OAT

TAB

VIE

4 Letters

ADAM

ALES

ARAM

ARIA

ARTS

BITE

BRAM

DIDO

GLAD

GOBI

GOBS

KLEE

LARA

MOPS

ODES

RANI

SEMI

TENT

5 Letters

LASTS

LIMED

MARIA

NASTY

SECTS

SIXTY

UNLIT

YEARN

YUMMY

6 Letters

ALCOVE

DILLON

ERRATA	PINATA	**7 Letters**
FEELER	REALMS	MUSICAL
GNOMES	RETAIL	NOSE BAG
NESTED	RIALTO	RELAYED
ONEIDA	SAILOR	SAMURAI
ORACLE	TALENT	

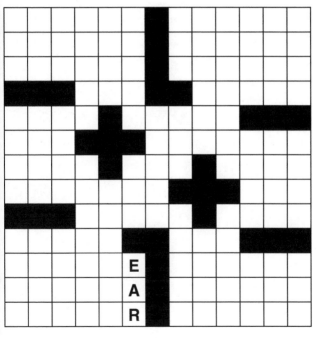

81

3 Letters

AGE

ALE

ALI

DUE

ERG

GOV.

MTV

NEE

OLE

REM

RON

RTE.

RUN

RUT

TUN

URN

USO

VIA

4 Letters

APSE

BYTE

CASE

EDDA

ELLA

ERAL

FLOP

IOWA

LOLL

LOPE

OVID

OWES

PAWS

REED

SCAD

SPEW

STAG

ST. LO

TAPA ✓

TELL

TIES

YVES

5 Letters

DAISY

EASEL

ENNUI

GEESE

HASTE

MEDAL

SERUM

WOVEN

6 Letters

ADMIRE

ATTEST

ELEVEN	DUCHESS	**8 Letters**
TRUDGE	FISHNET	ASSIGNED
	VANESSA	GEORGIAN
7 Letters	YODELED	NEW DELHI
BOREDOM		REGISTER
CASTILE		

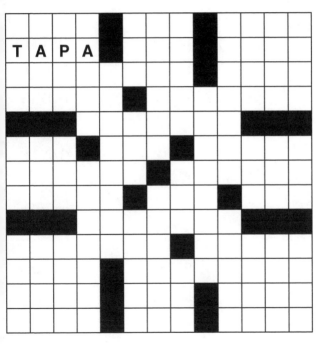

82

3 Letters

BOW

CRY

ELM

ETA

HEW

LAM

NAN

OIL

ORE

RCA

SST

STY

TAN

TOY

WOO

4 Letters

BOMB

BR'ER

DEAL ✓

DIPS

EGGY

ELUL

EMIT

ERIE

ESPY

MASH

OMAR

OMIT

PITA

ROTA

SEAN

SENT

TREY

WANE

5 Letters

ATRIA

DECOR

DERMA

DONDI

DOTTY

DWELT

GAYLE

LHASA

STELE

6 Letters

ADAGIO

ANGELA

ASPECT	MAY DAY	**8 Letters**	
EAGLET	ODDEST	DO-GOODER	
ENGINE	OODLES	EDGEWISE	
ISRAEL	ROOMER	IRONWEED	
LASERS	TWEEDS	THRILLED	
LEYDEN	YOGURT		

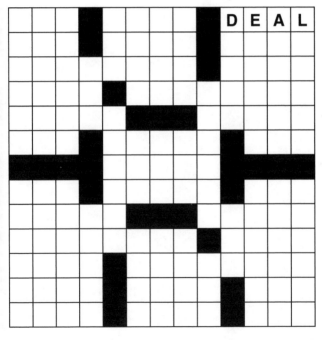

83

3 Letters

ADE
APO
ASP
CUR
ELK
ENG.
ERR
FRY
IRK
ONO
OWE
POE
PRY
PTA
Q.E.D.
RAH ✓
REO

RIO
TIN
TOO

4 Letters

AGNI
AMID
AWOL
BAHS
DUDE
DYED
EDDY
EGAD
EMIR
EPEE
EPOS
FREE
HOED
HOPE
ICON

IDEA
IN RE
IRAQ
IRMA
LIAR
MANY
NEAT
POGO
RATE
REEK
RING
RODS
RUGS
TONE
USES
YOGA
YOGI

5 Letters

EMBER

HAREM ETCHED **8 Letters**

OMEGA IODINE ADAPTING

SYNOD MYRIAD ANTEROOM

PACKET MEDIATOR

6 Letters

ELINOR RENDER PRIORITY

84

3 Letters

ADS
ANI
APT
ARC
AVA
AVE.
CAR
FEE
FUR
IKE
MOE
NAE
OWN
PEA
REE
SEW

UKE
WAF
WOE
YEW

4 Letters

ACES
ACHE
AGRA
ATTY.
AVAR
AVON
BAST
BRUT
DEER
DRAT ✓
ERST
EVER
GRAB

IVAN
KANE
KIWI
NARD
NASA
NESS
OBEY
RUSE
TERN
THEE
WADI
WATT
WORM

5 Letters

FISHY
LASSO
LATER
OASIS

SINEW

WANDA

6 Letters

ABBOTT

ARISEN

ARLENE

EEYORE

ENMESH

INDEED

ISLAND

NASSER

7 Letters

ANATOMY

RESOLES

REWARDS

SEALANT

85

3 Letters

ANN

COW

EDD

EGO

HOE

LIE

LOT

LTD.

MUG

OHM

ORO ✓

RPM

SGT.

4 Letters

AHAB

AIRS

ANON

BOOK

BOOT

BRED

DENY

DOME

GERM

HIND

HOBO

ICED

LAOS

LARD

ORDO

OUSE

PALL

PLAN

RITA

ROAN

ROIL

VAIN

5 Letters

ARGOT

ARIEL

GALAS

MOWED

NABOB

NONET

SHEIK

SHOVE

6 Letters

ABATED

BERING	PHRASE	**7 Letters**
DONATE	PROVEN	ATTESTS
LAMOUR	ROCOCO	AUDIBLY
LOOTED	SEETHE	DIE-HARD
ORIENT	TENTED	PROTEGE
OTIOSE		VITAMIN

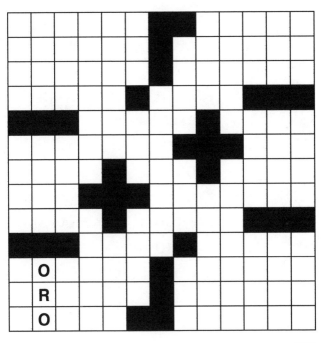

86

3 Letters

AUK

BAA

CEO

EAU

EDO

ELI

EST.

FUN

HAN

IRA

LOS

NAB

NET

PBS

RHO

SAG

SEA

SRO

TBA

UTE

4 Letters

AGEE

ALLY

APIA

ASTI

ATTU

BITE

DADO

DREG

EASE

EKED

ERGO

FADO

FIST

GEED

HEEP

LEFT

OATH

ODOR

OGEE

PATE

RIND

SCUD

TALC

TEND

TORN

YALU

5 Letters

ARUBA

BANAL

CREAK

EOSIN

LAURA ✓

LEASH

NIFTY

YUKON

6 Letters

BERATE

MOSAIC

REFORM

SEMPRE

TEEMED

TIGHTS

7 Letters

CALIPER

ISRAELI

RAINING

STETSON

LAURA

87

3 Letters

ALT.

BAR

BOP

CEE

EBO

HMO

ILL

OPE

ORT

RBI

SAC

TEA

4 Letters

ACID

ADDS ✓

AINU

ANAT.

CHAT

DATA

DHOW

EATS

ERSE

FLEE

GAGE

GRAD

IOTA

ISLE

LIRA

MEIR

NAES

OMEN

ONER

ONTO

OTIS

ROME

ROOF

STAY

SUDS

TENS

TUFT

USMA

5 Letters

AMBLE

APORT

EELER

RUBLE

6 Letters

AENEAS

		BOBBED		REPOSE			8 Letters

COILED   SHREWD   BROADWAY

BOBBED   REPOSE   **8 Letters**

COILED   SHREWD   BROADWAY

DEFEAT   SWEETS   FORETELL

ENRICO   TERESA   GLASSFUL

PALLET   TSETSE   RELATION

PELOTA

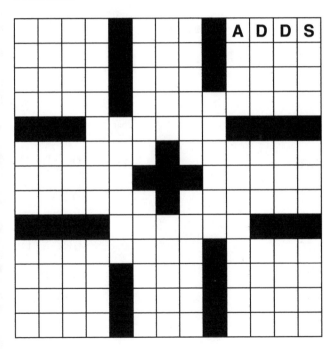

88

3 Letters

AWE
ELM
ENS
GAR
GOV.
HEP
IDA
IDS
IRE
ROE
SAL
SIC
TNT
YAK
YAW

4 Letters

AREA
ASPS
ATON
CODE
DORY
EROS
ITER
LENS
NAME
NODE
PARA
PLIE
RAKE
SATE
SNOW
WHOA

5 Letters

AEGIS
BASIN
DEPTH
EARTH
SASSY ✓
SEEMS
TEAMS
VENAL

6 Letters

DASHED
EMOTED
EREBUS
LEGATO
LEMMON
ORNERY
PILATE

POODLE

REOPEN

SCHEME

SEVERE

SHRIEK

STEELY

VIENNA

7 Letters

DYNASTY

KESTREL

KETTLES

SPEAKER

STRETCH

SUSPEND

TRIESTE

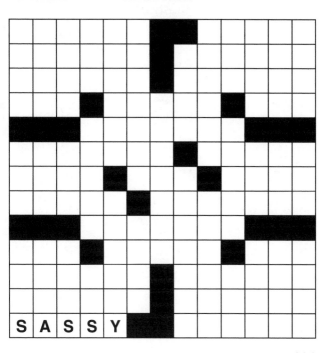

89

3 Letters

AMA

EKE

EMU

EON

IOU

LED

MUD

O'ER

ONE

PEN

POE

PRO

PUP

RAP

REM

ROC

TET

TKO

TOR

WPM

4 Letters

ABLE

ALEA

ASIA

AWED

BLOT

DADA

EDDA

ENID ✓

FALL

FINN

HERR

HIKE

IONA

IRON

I SEE

NAIF

NINA

OSLO

RISE

SHAH

SWAN

TEEN

VOID

WILE

5 Letters

ABIDE

A LIST

ANEAR

BRAIN

LEAFY

LILAC	**7 Letters**	**8 Letters**
MADAM	ETAMINE	LENIENCE
NAIVE	EYELASH	LIBRETTO
SISAL	ICELAND	MAPMAKER
TIBIA	MAHATMA	WILDWOOD

90

3 Letters

ADE
ATM
CUE
CUR
EVA
GEE
ICE
ION
KEY
PTA
SPA
TAO
TAU
VCR

184

4 Letters

ANOA
DAME
DEEP
DIRT
EDEN
ELAN
ELSA
ESTE
HERB
LIPS
NESS
ODES
ORES
PSST
STOP
TABS

5 Letters

AUDEN
ENATE
IDAHO
IRANI ✓
LEERY
NERVY
ORION
SATYR
T-BILL

6 Letters

ALLEGE
DACTYL
DEVISE
ELEVEN
ENCORE

EVERTS	OPENER	**7 Letters**
GANTRY	RIPEST	AMOROUS
MASSED	RUSTED	CANASTA
MERLIN	SLOGAN	INSTALL
MOANED	TIRADE	NIBLICK
NANTES		ROYALTY

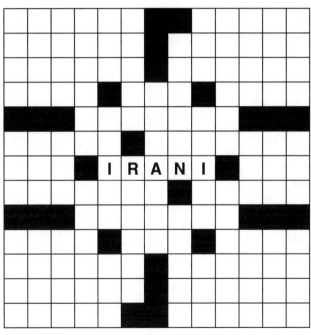

91

3 Letters

CPA
ERR
ETA
EWE
GAS
HEN
OTT
PAT
REO
SHY
SOB
SUB

4 Letters

AGNI

AIDA
BALI
CHIN
ELIS
ELUL
HALO
HAUL
HOAR
HOOP
HOST
IAGO
ILKA
NEON
OBIE
OBOE
POLL
PUNY
ROLE

SLUE ✓
SODA
SPAN
TBSP.
TEAM
THEY
TOYS
WIPE
YOKO

5 Letters

FLARE
OPENS
WATCH
YOUTH

6 Letters

ASSORT

BANGOR	ESTEEM	**8 Letters**
BISTRO	MASSES	CRYSTALS
BOMBAY	REAPER	ICE CREAM
CRAYON	REFINE	SOMEWHAT
DASHER	SCHISM	YIELDING
EGOISM		

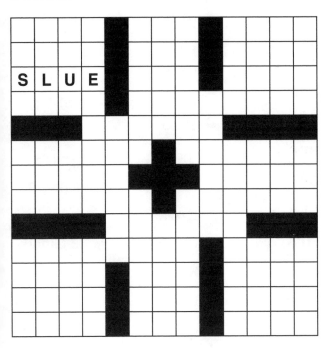

92

3 Letters

ABC

ABE

ACE

ALE

ANN ✓

ASH

BAA

BEE

BIT

EBB

MBA

MTV

RAF

RAN

TEN

TIC

4 Letters

ALEE

BEAR

DRIP

EMIT

ET AL.

EVEN

FLEA

GENT

HUGS

IOWA

IRAN

KURT

LENT

LETT

MA'AM

NOES

SEMI

SPAR

5 Letters

DELTA

EBONY

ERRED

ISLET

MAKER

PINTS

TEEMS

6 Letters

AERIAL

ALUMNA

ASPIRE

ASSIGN	METTLE	**7 Letters**
ENDEAR	OPENED	ARTEMIS
ESSENE	SENATE	ETERNAL
ETCHES	STEREO	OURSELF
GRETEL	WANDER	SIROCCO
HUMANE		STUPEFY

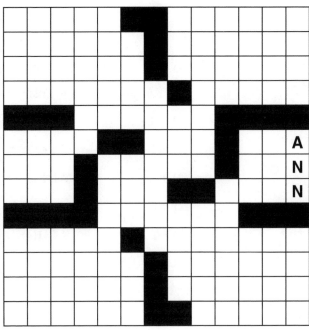

93

3 Letters

ATE
AVA
DAP
ELI
ERE
EVE
FOP
HAD
LTD.
NED
ORT
RAH
TAI
URI

190

4 Letters

ADDS
ALGA
ALSO
BOLT
DYED
ERST
IN RE
LIRA
MARE ✓
NOEL
OLAV
OVEN
REPO
RITA
RUNS
SARI
SPIN

TEEM

5 Letters

HEDDA
ITEMS
LAPSE
LEAVE
PLAYA
ROMAN
VAPID

6 Letters

ADRIFT
ALFRED
ATONED
BYE-BYE
ELATED
IGNITE

NASSER	THESES	GLEEFUL
OSIRIS	URBANE	LITTLER
PARODY		REGATTA
PLURAL	**7 Letters**	SETTLED
REINED	DEPOSIT	UTTERLY
TAYLOR	ELDERLY	

94

3 Letters

AHA

AIL

ARE

AWN

BAM

DAL

I'VE

LAD

RTE.

SGT.

4 Letters

ADEN

AMEN

ANNE

APIA

BESS

BRAE

EARL

ELSE

GNAT

LANI

OMEN

ORAL

RAIL

RAYE

RENO

RUBY

SMEE

STAY ✓

STEM

TAXI

TWOS

WITS

5 Letters

ADDAX

AORTA

BEARS

ELMAN

ENACT

LISZT

NONET

TASTY

TONGA

6 Letters

ALLURE

AT HOME

DRAMAS

6 Letters		7 Letters
EMBRYO	MODEST	**7 Letters**
ENERGY	NEATLY	APTNESS
ENTAIL	SALIVA	CARDOZO
IMBIBE	STYLED	OPINION
LEADED	WAMPUM	RATTLER
MEDUSA		SEDATED

95

3 Letters

AID
DOT
EDD
EDO
EGO
ELD
ELK
ELL
ESP
HEP
IRA
POE
RNA
TAN
UTE

4 Letters

ACED
ADAM
AGIO
AMAH
DOLE
EDIE
ELMO
ERLE
FLED
LAKE
NELL
NOSH
OLGA
SEAL
SEAM
STOL
TALC
UGLI

5 Letters

EARTH
ENTER
NEPAL ✓
PEALE
POSSE
STRAP

6 Letters

ADAGIO
AGOUTI
AMANDA
APOLLO
ARENAS
COHERE
DAPPER
EL TORO

INSECT

LISTEN

NEATER

PREENS

REGRET

REHEAT

REPOSE

TORPID

7 Letters

ETAMINE

GONDOLA

MOMENTO

NEEDFUL

PRAISED

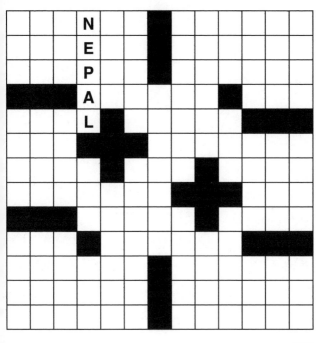

3 Letters

AVE.

BEA

DEN

DIN

EKE

ENG.

GET

GIN

KEY ✓

MED.

OTO

ROM

SIS

TAC

TAO

4 Letters

ANTE

AXEL

BLAT

DRYS

EONS

ETRE

EXAM

GREY

IDLE

JACK

JADE

LEAR

MAYS

MEMO

OLEO

POST

RANI

TEMP

5 Letters

EARNS

ERECT

ESSEN

OPINE

PLEBE

RENEE

6 Letters

ADRIAN

AVALON

CLENCH

EDGIER

ENESCO

ENTERS LEVANT **7 Letters**

IAMBIC PLATTE EERIEST

JIGGLE PRESTO ENHANCE

KEENAN REEVES GESTALT

LACIER TSETSE MAJORCA

LARIAT MEANEST

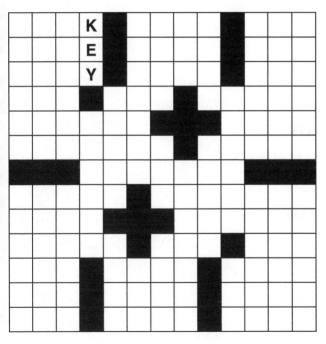

3 Letters

ARM

DAY

E'EN

ERA

ERR

FEY

HOP

KIT

NAN

NEE

NOR

OAK

OTT

RAE

REE

ROD

RYE

SIC

TBA

USN

4 Letters

ADIT

ALDO

ARTS

ASTA

DELE

DENT

DORA

DYNE

EDDY

EKES

ESPY

ISLE

ISN'T

LANA

LIEN

POSE

ROUE

SCAB

SEEP

TAUT

TESS

YAPS

5 Letters

EATEN

ETHAN

FETED ✓

FORTH

FREUD

OKAPI

SCALP

TAUPE	ATTIRE	SIERRA
TERRY	AURORA	TENTER
TRACE	EARNED	UNEASE
	NETTED	UNREEL
6 Letters	RAINED	YEARLY
ANTHEM	SEARED	

98

3 Letters

ADS

ALI

ALT. ✓

AMT.

COO

ELY

ETA

HAL

IRE

MOA

ODE

SEA

TOO

VEE

200

4 Letters

ADES

ASST.

AVIS

ENDS

ERRS

ESTE

EWER

GOAT

ICES

IVAN

KNEE

METE

NIKE

OKRA

ONES

REVS

SERE

VOTE

5 Letters

AIDED

ARISE

DREAD

INDIA

NEATH

NEGEV

OSAGE

TESTY

TRESS

6 Letters

ARRAYS

DRIVER

ELEVEN	SLEEVE	**7 Letters**
ENMESH	SLOWER	ADMIRAL
GASKET	SOCKET	BRISTOL
IRONED	STEELE	CASHIER
KRAMER	WIZARD	RAREBIT
REZONE	YAWNED	SAVARIN

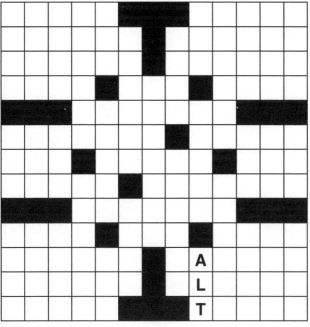

99

3 Letters

BIT

COB

ENS

ERE

GNP

INN

LEI

NIB

OLE

OWL

RUM

SOD

SPY

URI

YIP

4 Letters

CHIC

CREW

DRIP

DYED

EBBS ✓

EBRO

EDNA

EGGS

GALL

NILE

OLIO

OMAR

PROD

REAL

ROUT

ST. LO

5 Letters

BEBOP

DAUBS

FREED

LADLE

OMEGA

SCOOT

STAIR

STAND

6 Letters

ACACIA

ADESTE

CLUBBY

ECLAIR

FLORID

GODIVA

GUNNER

HOMBRE

LEASES

NIELLO

PROVED

SCREAM

TAILED

TRENDY

7 Letters

ANTIQUE

CONCERT

MYSTERY

PUNGENT

QUALITY

STENCIL

TROUNCE

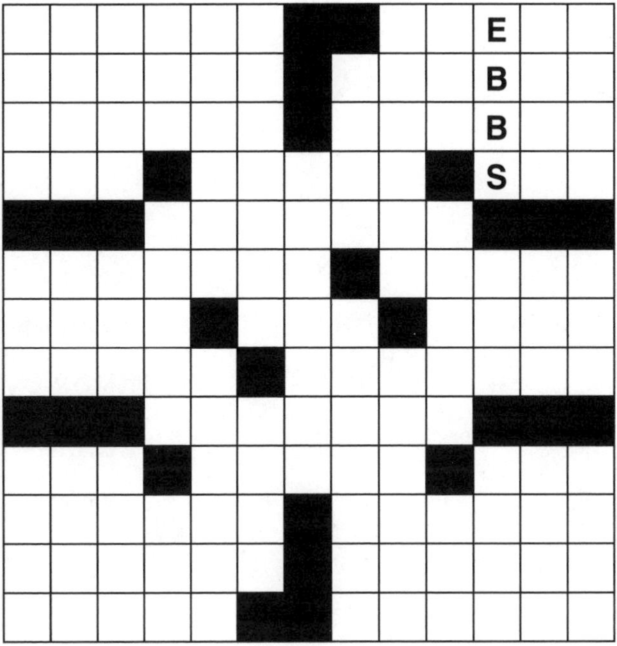

100

3 Letters

ACT
ANA
ANN
HEY
ION
LEE
LI'L
NAE
NET
ONE
ONO
SAC
SOB
TOT

204

4 Letters

AGEE
ALAR
APER ✓
DEAR
DUAL
EARL
EASE
ELLA
ESNE
ETNA
INCA
REAR
REST
SEEK
SWAP
TRIP

5 Letters

ELENA
IDEAL
LEASH
SHEER
SPATE
TABOO
TAPED
TWEET
VISOR

6 Letters

ANDREW
ARARAT
ARLENE
ASLEEP
CANALS

ENCINA	PLAYED	**7 Letters**
ENRAGE	REESES	ARTISAN
FACADE	SIFTER	AVERRED
HOARSE	TESTER	ERRATIC
NUTRIA	WALLOP	TASTIER
OAKLEY		TENANCY

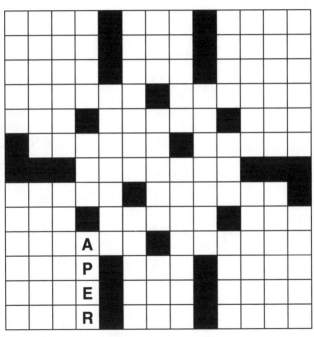

101

3 Letters

ADE

AFT ✓

ARF

CNN

EOS

ESP

HUT

IOU

LEO

LON

REB

REO

TED

VIA

4 Letters

ACRE

AIRS

ALOE

AREA

BODE

CABS

CLUE

COAX

DENS

IBID.

IGOR

I SEE

KLEE

PINT

RUST

RYAN

TAXI

TEST

5 Letters

ALLOW

CRACK

DYERS

ENERO

ESTOP

NOLTE

OWNER

PACER

ROAST

6 Letters

ENRICO

IRONER

LAUREN	OUTFIT	**7 Letters**
NEARBY	RETIRE	CONIFER
OBSESS	STEREO	FINLAND
OCEANS	STOOGE	FONSECA
O'NEILL	TENDON	NINEVEH
ONIONY	UNTRUE	TRENTON

102

3 Letters

ALF

ALL

AMP

A-OK

EMS

FOB

GUT

IRS

LEA

ODA

OPT

ORE

TAU

TEA

UTE

4 Letters

ADEN

ALUM

ANAT.

DATA

D-DAY

ERST

LOOP

MERE ✓

OLES

OSLO

OTTO

PSST

TEEM

TICS

ULNA

USED

5 Letters

ALOUD

CASTE

DRAIN

FATES

HIDES

OLEIN

RESTS

SIFTS

STAKE

TENET

6 Letters

ADHERE

AWHILE

CANOLA

CHALET

ETUDES

INLAID   SESTET   OVERAGE

METERS   TORRID   REYNARD

NIECES   TOSSED   SNORTED

OCTAVE   SWEETEN

ODESSA   **7 Letters**

ONEIDA   BLATANT

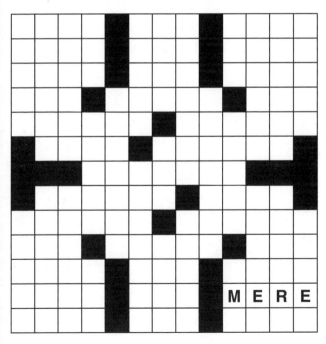

103

3 Letters

AAH
ART
BAY
EAR
ETC.
HEP
LYE
OAK
OIL
PBS
RBI
TAG
TBA
TIC

4 Letters

ADIT
AIRE
ARES
CREE
ERLE
EURO
FETE
IMAM ✓
IN RE
JELL
MELT
MIKE
NOAH
RIFF
SCAM
SEAM
STAB
THEM

5 Letters

AMEND
BEECH
CHEST
EDITH
ERATO
HONES
LEHAR
RIANT
SKEIN

6 Letters

AERIAL
ATTIRE

EEYORE	NINETY	**7 Letters**		
FRINGE	OYSTER	ADJOURN		
IAMBIC	SNITCH	APRICOT		
INDIAN	TOUCAN	COASTAL		
NEEDED	TRIBAL	POLYMER		
NICKEL	UPSALA	TADPOLE		

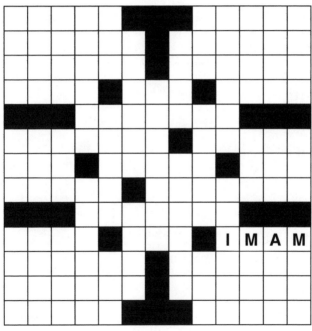

104

3 Letters

ACE

CEE

COO

EGG

IDA

LEN

MID

NEO

ORO

SOL

4 Letters

BATT

BEST

EERY

ENOW

ERSE

ETRE

EYRE ✓

HAIG

INKY

IRON

KNIT

KNOW

LORI

MODE

NORA

NOSY

OGEE

PEEN

SEER

STAR

TACO

TANS

UTES

VALE

5 Letters

ARTEL

ASNER

IRKED

NORTH

O'NEAL

6 Letters

ABBOTT

ANIMAL

ATTACK

ESCAPE

GLOBES

GOOBER	SWEDEN	**7 Letters**
IDEATE	TERSER	AVENGER
LANCER	TOTALS	EGOTISM
NOVICE	TRALEE	SNEAKER
RELIVE	VIRTUE	VILLAGE
RENNET		WANTING

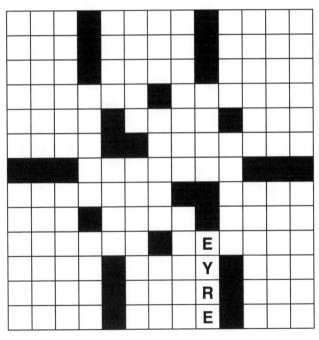

105

3 Letters

APT

AWE

COB

FEE

MAP

O'ER

ORO

PIN

RIM

SLY

SOX

SRO

'TIS ✓

WAD

4 Letters

ATTU

AVAR

EARP

FUEL

FUME

GRAB

HERA

MUIR

NERO

ORCA

OTTO

ROMP

SHEM

USMA

VANS

WACO

5 Letters

AFTON

MACAW

NIECE

SITAR

STONY

YUMMY

6 Letters

ACTION

ARETHA

ELAPSE

EMILIO

ENTAIL

LARYNX

MOROSE

PEORIA

POTTER	**8 Letters**	ROSSETTI
SOCCER	ADORNING	SISTERLY
TERCET	ATALANTA	TORMENTS
TRAITS	ICE CREAM	
USURPS	POSITIVE	
VOTERS	RETRENCH	

3 Letters

AGE

AGO

ARC

ARM

DEB

EAR ✓

ERE

ESP

GAL

JOT

MAR

ODE

TEN

YEN

4 Letters

ABBR.

ASEA

ASST.

BARB

BIAS

CANE

DARE

ERGS

ESTE

ETUI

ODIN

REIN

ROSA

ROTE

TEND

TERN

5 Letters

ALLIE

GRIPE

LEDGE

ORSON

RETRO

SEPAL

TORTE

6 Letters

ADESTE

AMENDS

ARRIVE

ASSORT

BATHES

BRUINS

GYRATE

INSERT	RIBBON	ESSENCE
IRVING	SHINTO	INTEGER
ISOBAR	STANCE	MAJORCA
RAIDER		PLIABLE
REESES	**7 Letters**	SNAPPED
RESCUE	ALGERIA	TONNEAU

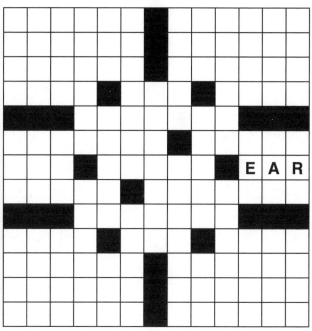

3 Letters

ADE ✓

BYE

EGO

ELL

EVA

GEL

IRA

I'VE

KOS

LAD

PEN

REE

REO

SOD

URI

VEG

WAR

YEW

4 Letters

AGIO

ARIL

BAIL

BR'ER

CAST

DRAW

EELY

ELKS

ENOS

EVIL

FELL

GANT

INCA

INDY

IRON

LOAD

NINO

OBIE

OGRE

ORAL

RAKE

RARE

RICH

TANK

TWIG

TYPO

URAN

YELL

5 Letters

CLARA

LEAVE

LIANA

LODEN

WYATT

XERIC

6 Letters

ATTUNE

ELANDS

ETHNIC

NEARLY

ROTATE

TROWEL

7 Letters

EXCERPT

FALSELY

IRELAND

TORRENT

UPSCALE

VOYAGED

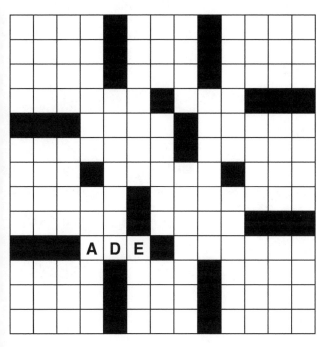

3 Letters

AID

AMP

APO

BOW

DEE

ELF

ELY

ENG.

ENS

LEE ✓

NEO

ORE

OUR

REB

SAG

TIC

4 Letters

ALDO

ANTE

AVON

BOLA

DIAL

EASE

EDEN

EDGY

EPEE

ERRS

ETON

EWER

FRET

ICON

LEVI

MEIR

OREL

OTIS

POCO

RAZE

RELY

ROBE

SANE

SANG

USES

WARD

WEED

ZERO

5 Letters

ACRES

BRAVA

ERASE

ERWIN

OARED

OVERT	BLAZON	NORDIC
URIEL	BRASSY	SIERRA
ZEBRA	COBRAS	TERESA
	INSURE	TSETSE
6 Letters	NITWIT	URSINE
AUSTIN	NOBLES	

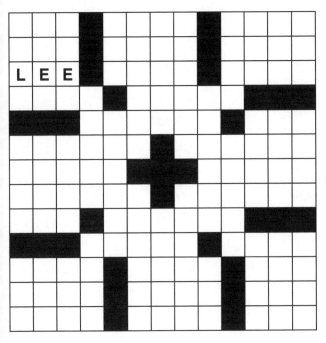

109

3 Letters

AAH
AKA
ASH
DAN
EOS
ERR
EST.
ETA
HER
IKE
IOU
LET
LIE
MAE
NOR
OTO

SIR
SOL
TAI
TIE

4 Letters

ALAN
ALES
ALIT
ANTS ✓
ASTI
DRAM
ESPY
ILKA
IONA
LONI
MATT
NOSH
OLLA
ONES

POLO
PUTT
RIAL
ROSE
ROUE
SINE
SKIP
STOP
TYPE
UPON

5 Letters

BLESS
EMEND
IRATE
LAPIN
NEHRU
SONES
TEETH
TUTOR

6 Letters

APOLLO

DIPPER

EATING

OWLISH

RIPEST

UMLAUT

7 Letters

DIAGRAM

IRIDIUM

NATURAL

NUMERAL

NURTURE

WASHTUB

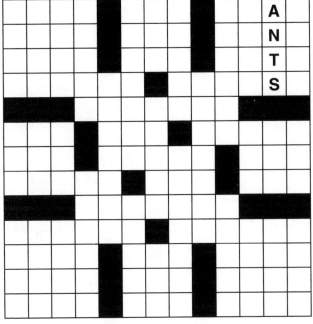

110

3 Letters

ALL

ANA

ARE

ATE

CAP

CEO

CUR

EDO

EON

ESS

GEM

ION

NAP

OLD

PEP

PUN

ROT

RTE.

SEA

YON

4 Letters

ABBE

ACES

AMES

ANIL

ARLO

BART

BONO

BRAY

COKE

CONE

DOTE

EIRE

ELAN

ELIA

ELSA ✓

ELSE

ELUL

ESAU

ESNE

ODDS

REPS

SECT

5 Letters

AGAPE

APSES

ASNER

DEPOT

ERROL

KITED

KUDZU

OASIS	ALTERS	ONEIDA
PLEBE	BRUTUS	REHEAT
RAJAH	CAJOLE	TIPTOP
	CARRIE	URANIC
6 Letters	DARKEN	ZAGREB
ALIENS	GUITAR	

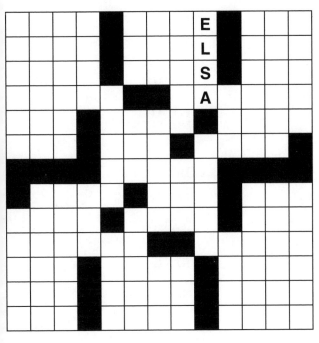

111

3 Letters

ALT.

ATM

BEA

CPA

EMU

HAN

PAL

REF

RUN

SST

SUP ✓

UHF

UMP

4 Letters

AMOK

CHAR

DEER

DYNE

EATS

EBAN

EERY

ELMO

ET AL.

LAPP

LEAF

MENU

PROA

RINK

SNAP

ULNA

5 Letters

ANKLE

EPEES

LUMEN

MEDEA

SEEMS

SENOR

6 Letters

AGREED

ANNALS

ELECTS

ERASES

ESTHER

FAUCET

GENTLE

GRASSO

IPECAC	ROTTEN	KOREANS
KEENAN	TREBLE	PEN NAME
LEADEN		RHOMBUS
MADAME	**7 Letters**	SMEARED
ODDITY	ANTIGUA	YASHMAK
REDEEM	ESPOUSE	

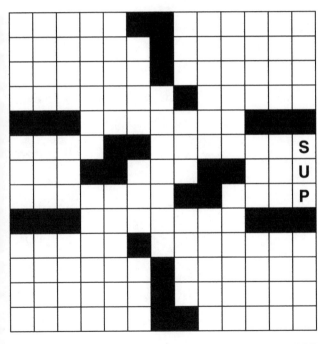

112

3 Letters

AMI
EAR
FRA
HOE
LOP
NEE
O'ER
OFF
ONE
ORO
PRO
SEC
THY
YET

4 Letters

AIDA
ALOE
ANAT.
ARIA
DADE
DEAL
EARL
IMAM ✓
LIED
MESS
MINE
NEAT
NODE
OSLO
RITA
SEAL
STAG

TENN.

5 Letters

BACON
CARTS
EASEL
EGYPT
ODETS
OPERA
TARES

6 Letters

ARDENT
ARENAS
EDITOR
ELIDED
GLADES
GLIDED

IODINE	TRENDS	GHASTLY
MILLED	UNTOLD	INSTALL
NOTICE		MIGRATE
PERSIA	**7 Letters**	OBLIGED
REELED	ASSORTS	UPRIGHT
TAILOR	FORMOSA	

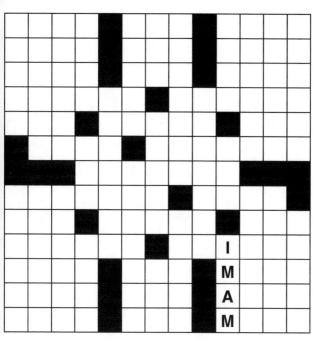

113

3 Letters

ADE
COO
DIT
EBO
ERA
EVE
FAR
GEE ✓
GEL
IRE
LEG
LOG
NAE
OBI
ODA
OLE

RAG
SAL
UFO
USA

4 Letters

ALEE
APER
ARMS
DESI
DOVE
EGAN
EPOS
GOAL
LARA
MAGI
NANA
OLGA
OPEN
ORAD

PURR
RAPT
ROLL
SAGO
SEIS
SLAP
VOID
WRAP
YALU
YODA

5 Letters

ICIER
INGOT
LINDA
O'HARE
ROGER
TAINT
TULIP
WYATT

6 Letters

AGOUTI

ESSENE

HALLEY

INDEED

LITTER

NELSON

7 Letters

AVAILED

EERIEST

GALLEON

ISOTONE

NEATEST

TSARINA

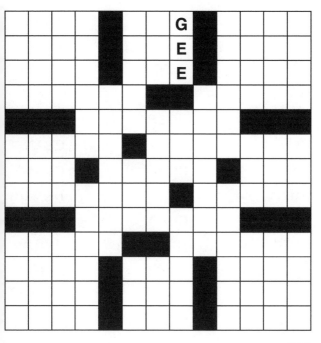

114

3 Letters

AGO
ART
CON
DAW
EGO
GAR
ICE
LOU
LYE
NYE
OHM
OIL
OOH
POD
ROE ✓
ROW

RYA
UPI
WOW
YIP

4 Letters

AERO
ALTO
ARNE
BR'ER
CHUG
COBS
COMO
CRAG
ERST
GOON
HIRE
HOOT
IDOL
MOMS

ODOR
OISE
OLIO
OTTO
PATH
PLOT
REEK
RENO
TITO
USED

5 Letters

CLANG
CLOMP
DEMUR
ELIHU
RYDER
SEDAN
STARS
TEACH

6 Letters

CARREL

GERALD

HARKEN

POORLY

SPLICE

UPROOT

7 Letters

ARCHAIC

LEISURE

NEUTRAL

PARSNIP

PRODUCT

ROASTER

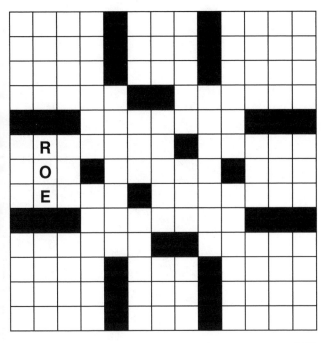

115

3 Letters

ABC
AHA
AKA
ALE
ALI
AMP
CAR
DEE
DOT
ELI
ETC.
IRA
LEN
NOB
OWN

POI
PSI
RES
TAT
TOW

4 Letters

ALAR
ASPS
BRED
DIVE
EDDY
EKED
ESTE
EZRA
LADD
NAIF
NARY
NENE ✓

NERO
OLAV
ONTO
REPO
RETE
ROAD
RUSS
SEEM
SEMI
TBSP.

5 Letters

ADOPT
ASWAN
DEBAR
EMERY
MARIA
OATEN
ODDER

5 Letters	ELUDER	SORTIE
REEDY	FEDORA	STAPLE
STRIP	ICEMAN	STEELE
ZEBRA	IRONIC	UNLOAD
	NATURE	WHALER
6 Letters	PERSON	
DECODE		

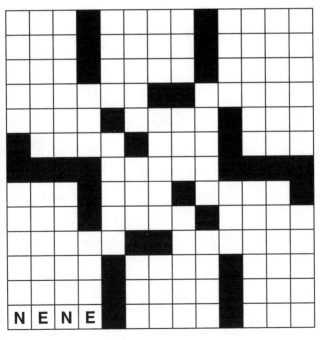

116

3 Letters

ARM

CAM

DEN

ETA

FEZ

ITS

PEA

POE

REE

SHY

STY

TAM

TET

UNO

4 Letters

ALAE

A LOT

AMAT

BRAM

EARP

EELY ✓

FAIR

GREY

HEMS

HOBO

ITCH

MIME

NEIL

NEST

OMAN

OURS

RETS

ROIL

SAFE

SARA

SPCA

SPUR

TIME

TIRE

TYRE

UTAH

5 Letters

BLUER

CRUDE

ELEMI

LLAMA

MAPLE

NICHE

6 Letters	OOLONG	HEARTILY
CAESAR	TYPING	IDOLATRY
CARRIE	ZYDECO	SPROUTED
COARSE		UMBRELLA
FIRING	**8 Letters**	YAMMERED
HEROIC	ALIENATE	

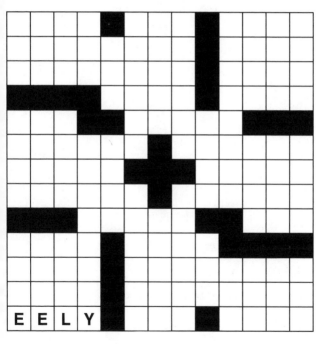

117

3 Letters

ACE
AMT.
BOG
DOE
EDO
ELK
ERE
ERR
FIR
HUN
LED
LES ✓
MOI
PET
REO

RIO
SEA
TSP.

4 Letters

AGED
AGIO
AGNI
AHEM
ANNE
EBAN
ERMA
ERSE
KNIT
LENO
LOGO
LOSE
MATE
NEAP

NOTE
ONER
OOPS
PAIR
PALE
REED
SENT
SNAP
TEAR
USMA

5 Letters

LATIN
NIECE
ORSON
PRIOR
PROSE
REALM

	6 Letters	ODESSA	CLEANSER
	AFLOAT	POTION	INNOCENT
	ATONED	TREATY	NOONTIME
	BETRAY		SHOEHORN
	GRASSO	**8 Letters**	TSARINAS
	NORMAL	BONDSMEN	

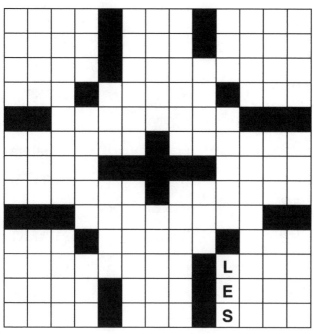

3 Letters

AAH

AVA

CHE

DAB

EAR

EDD

ENS

GAL

LAG

NET

ODD

SAW

VAN

VAT

240

4 Letters

ALEF

CADE

DEAL

EDDA

ET AL.

ETNA

EWER

IN RE

KINE

LIST

LOCH

NEVE

NINE ✓

RARE

REEL

SEAR

SKID

YARE

5 Letters

COSTA

DEFER

ELTON

OPALS

SECCO

SKEIN

STINT

6 Letters

ACTIVE

ADHERE

ARARAT

CRAVAT

DECLAW

GLANCE

6 Letters		
HEREBY	PSYCHE	GLUTTON
INNATE	UGANDA	ICED TEA
ITALIC		THROATY
KITTEN	**7 Letters**	VOLTAGE
LARIAT	ADVISED	WREATHS
ONEIDA	CAREENS	

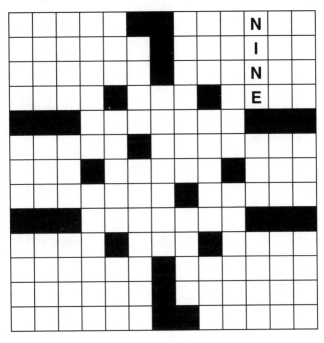

3 Letters

AGE

ANA

ESS

EST.

EWE

FIN

HIE

IVY

LEO

LOS

OWL

RNA

TOO

VIE ✓

WAS

YAM

4 Letters

ANNA

AVID

CLEF

ECRU

EKES

EROS

EXAM

GENE

GOES

HISS

INCA

IOWA

IVES

LEVI

LOLA

MA'AM

OVEN

OWEN

SAIL

SIGH

SLOG

STEW

TANG

TEDS

TIDE

VISA

X-RAY

YETI

5 Letters

ALIKE

AMINO

AMUSE

HUNCH

LEVEE

LIVER	CREATE	ISOBAR
SCRUB	ETUDES	SAUNAS
TESLA	EVADED	SEAVER
	EVERTS	SEETHE
6 Letters	HEAVES	SESTET
CLOVEN	INCHON	

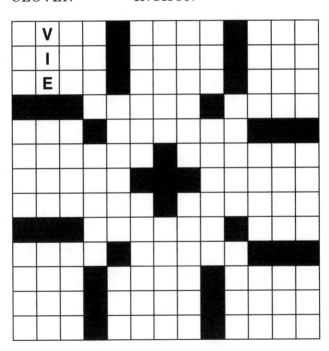

3 Letters

ADD
ADE
ADZ
ARE
ASP
BEE
EEK
EGG
ERA
ESP
HER
IKE
MRS.
NEO
NOT

ORE
RAD
SAD
SEE
UKE

4 Letters

AFAR
ARAS
ASTA
EGOS ✓
ELSE
ENID
EYER
LEIS
LESS
LUTE
MADE
MENU

NYPD
OMEN
OPAH
ORAL
RENT
SERB
SKYE
SLUE
TARA
VEAL

5 Letters

ABASE
BUNNY
DOUSE
EELER
GAYLE
LODGE
OILED

PAY-TV AURORA IRISES

SAVOR DAMAGE REARED

SLADE DEALER SILENT

DEPLOY ULTIMO

6 Letters DESIGN ZOYSIA

ANGELA FLAVOR

3 Letters

AHA

FLO

HAD

ION

IRA

LIE

OAR ✓

RAH

THE

TOT

TSK

URI

USO

WAR

4 Letters

AGIN

ANKH

ARNE

AVIS

BURN

EAVE

ESTE

GAPS

ICES

I SEE

LEGS

NODS

ONES

PLUS

REST

RETE

RIPE

RUIN

5 Letters

EDILE

ENSUE

ESSEN

FERAL

ISLES

NORTH

TRAIL

6 Letters

ALLURE

AVERSE

EARFUL

ECLAIR

EL PASO

EL TORO

FRIEND	TEUTON	LAUGHED
GRAPPA	VISION	LENTILS
IDEATE		NEITHER
NOTING	**7 Letters**	STELLAR
SIPPED	DEBASER	TWIDDLE
TEASES	EASIEST	

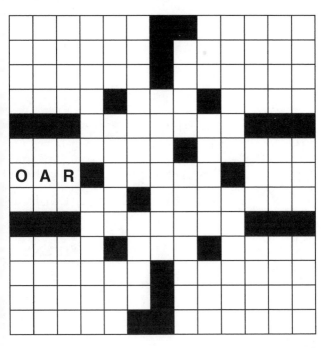

122

3 Letters

ALP
ANI
APT
BAA
BOO
GEL
GET
GUT
IRE
JOT
LEG ✓
LUG
ONE
OTT
OUI
REC.

REX
SIB
SLY
VIA

4 Letters

APIA
ARCS
AS IF
ASST.
BEYS
COPE
EPEE
ETUI
GEES
GNAT
GOAL
INGE
JURY
NENE

OPAL
PYLE
RHEA
RING
SCAR
SIRE
SNUG
TALL
TAME
TERM
TYNE
URAN

5 Letters

FELIX
GIVER
IRENE
SUGAR
TEASE
URIAH

6 Letters

BOLERO

CASEIN

LENNON

MAGNET

NUGGET

SYRUPY

7 Letters

EASTMAN

LITURGY

NOSE BAG

OUTLINE

RUPTURE

UPSCALE

123

3 Letters

ADS

APT

COT

EBO

GAS

LUG

O'ER

OLE

OPE

PTA ✓

RAD

RTE.

TSK

USO

VHS

4 Letters

ANIL

ASAP

ASKS

BAIT

EELY

GINA

ISN'T

KRIS

LIRA

SCAD

SECT

SNAP

TAPA

TARA

TUBA

VOTE

5 Letters

ADELA

APSES

DAVID

ITALY

MACRO

RAPID

SEDER

TULSA

6 Letters

AISLES

ANORAK

ASSUME

BAILEY

BASICS

BERATE

DESALT

EMERGE	TANDEM	IGNITED
ETHNIC	UNROLL	ORDERED
		PIEBALD
RANGER		PROTEGE
	7 Letters	
RAVINE	ARBITER	YIELDED
	DERANGE	
TAILED		

124

3 Letters

ALE

ASP

CHE

CPO

ELI

ELM

ERA

ETA

HEN

HUH

NCO

ODE

OWE

REC.

REE

TNT

TOT

4 Letters

AHEM

APEX

ELSA

EPEE ✓

ESTE

EWER

GLUT

LETT

OOZE

OXEN

RENT

SOAP

SOHO

SUMO

TEEN

TEMP

WHAT

YSER

YULE

ZEES

5 Letters

APORT

ATTIC

DELFT

EAGLE

FIONA

LADEN

NERVE

PETIT

VALET

WYATT	EQUITY	PLUMES
XENON	EVERTS	POLITE
	EXTENT	SAHARA
6 Letters	OMELET	SEQUEL
ADESTE	ORIOLE	SPLINT
CLEAVE	PATTER	TEUTON

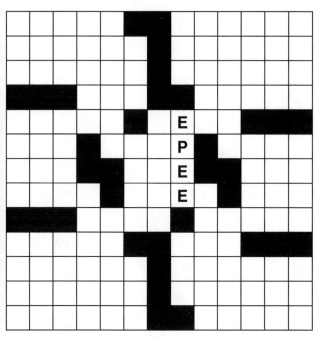

125

3 Letters

ALY
BLT
COY
DEW
EDD
EEL
ERR
FED
FRY
IDS
MEL
MET
MOA
NAE
OOH

PGA
RCA
TAV
UFO
WHO

4 Letters

ALPS
ANTE
ASTA
BOSH
EASE
ENVY
HEDY
HIES
HORN
IDEA
ISLE
LESS

LOCO
MOOT
MORN
OMAR
OVAL
PORE
SEAL
SOME ✓
THOR
VASE

5 Letters

AYRES
IBSEN
KARMA
PALER
ROCKY
ROSIN
SCOUR

SCUFF	COBWEB	HOOFER
STAYS	CRISPS	IMMUNE
UDDER	DEGREE	IMPAIR
	DOODAD	RESALE
6 Letters	EMBODY	UNWARY
ARNESS	ERODED	

126

3 Letters

ABS

ASK

ATM

BAA

EAU

ELL ✓

EON

ERE

EWE

GAT

MAR

MAY

ORE

RAE

RUM

SEE

SPA

UKE

URN

WOK

4 Letters

AKIN

ALEA

ALVA

ANAT.

ASEA

ASHE

BAWL

DIRK

EAST

ENDS

FAUN

GIDE

ITEM

ITER

LANI

LENA

NEWT

REEL

REST

ROBS

URDU

YARE

5 Letters

ABATE

DAMES

ERWIN

INERT

ISLET

NYLON

SKEET

SMELT	ANNALS	GARAGE
U-TURN	ARGYLE	ISOBAR
WHIST	AROUND	PROVED
	BUREAU	SAMUEL
6 Letters	DEBATE	SULLEN
ANGELS	FINALE	

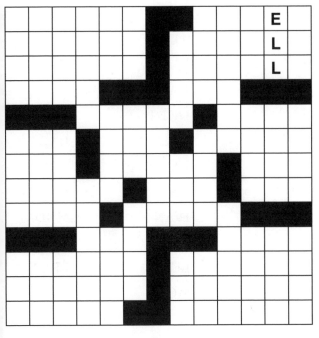

127

3 Letters

AAH
AHA
AND
ART
ENG.
ESP
EVA
GAM
GNU
HOP
MAP
NOR
OAR
ODD
ONE
RAN
RHO
ROE
RYA
SON

4 Letters

AGOG
AIRE
ALEC
BLUE
DAME
DUET
ERST
I-BAR
IGOR
IVAN
LENO
LOTS
MONA
MORK
MOTH
NINO
OLLA
ORAN
OVEN
OVID
RATE
REND ✓
RENO
RIVE

5 Letters

EAGER
ERROR
KNOLL
MEDAL
NEGEV
PRUNE
REARM
TERRA

6 Letters

ADDLED

APIECE

DERAIL

DILUTE

IODIDE

NAUGHT

7 Letters

ASTRIDE

EARNEST

EVIDENT

GOOD-BYE

LABELED

PERVADE

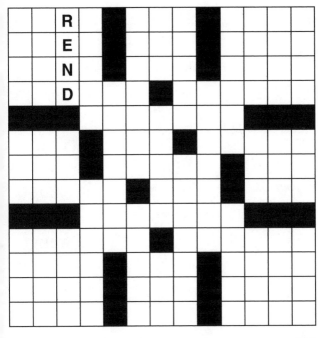

3 Letters

ADE

AIM

ANN

ATE ✓

AWE

BIO

DAN

DYE

IAN

IOU

LOP

LOU

NBA

OUR

PUN

SIB

SIX

TET

4 Letters

ACED

ALOE

ARNE

ASST.

ATON

CHAT

CURE

DAMP

EDIE

EPIC

HALE

HATH

LAVE

LIED

LUNA

NENE

NEXT

ONER

OPUS

PADS

ROTA

SCAR

SLOE

TEND

TIRE

UTAH

VAST

WISP

5 Letters

ALDER

CRUET

REEVE

SALVE

TAROT

WORST

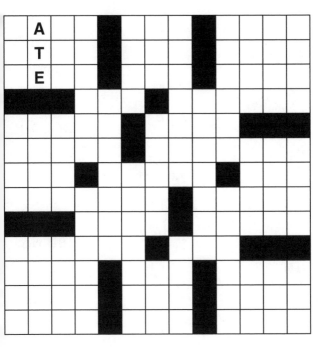

3 Letters

ACT

BUN

CUE

EEK

ELY

EMS

GAD

GOT

LET

MEG

OBI

TIM

VAT

VEE

VIA

YET

4 Letters

ASTI

COAL

EDGE

EDNA

RAYE

SANE

5 Letters

DEEDS

LIMBS

PENCE

READE

SHIRK

STEVE ✓

SYNOD

VERGE

6 Letters

AGOUTI

ASSESS

CHANEL

DEVOTE

EAGLET

ENCODE

ENGAGE

ENTERS

GRADED

IBERIA

IGUANA

LARGER

LINAGE

6 Letters		
MINING	SLEETS	ENAMELS
MONDAY	TINGLE	ESSENCE
PRIORY	TOPPLE	GENERAL
ROUTER		IRELAND
RUNNER	**7 Letters**	TRAILER
SELDOM	CISTERN	

130

3 Letters

AMA

ARM

BAH

E'EN

MIN.

NAG

ORO

OUT

POP

RED ✓

RNA

SAT

SIR

SKY

STY

4 Letters

ALDA

ASIA

BIBB

BOSS

CIAO

DADE

DENT

ENOS

ERIK

NOEL

OBIE

OMAN

PAGE

RAGA

ROME

ROSA

TECH

WREN

5 Letters

ABETS

DANES

EARLE

ELATE

NASAL

RABAT

REALM

TENSE

6 Letters

ABRADE

CERISE

DAMONE

DIETER	MEDUSA	HISTORY
DOWSES	OOLONG	PANACEA
DYNAST	STEADY	SERAPES
EDENIC		SLATHER
EDISON	**7 Letters**	STREETS
IAMBIC	DIPLOMA	YIELDED

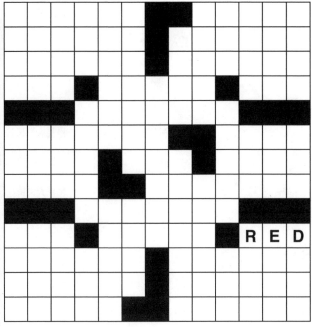

131

3 Letters

AVE.

DEN

IRA

IRE

I'VE

KIP

LEE

LON

NAN

NED

PEN

RAH

ROC

WIT

4 Letters

ARIA

ASKS

EATS

ERIN

EURO

GILD

LAND

ORES ✓

ORTS

RENT

SAGA

SINK

STEP

STOL

TUNA

USAF

5 Letters

ETAPE

IOWAN

MEESE

NIECE

OPINE

PENDS

TREND

6 Letters

DRAPED

EILEEN

ERASER

ERODED

IDEATE

INTENT

NATANT

6 Letters		

ONIONY   THEFTS   KINDEST

OPPOSE   TRIPLE   ONTARIO

PADDED   TURRET   PERCENT

PEORIA   RECITED

POTATO   **7 Letters**   RETIRED

STEEDS   EMINENT   STYLIST

132

3 Letters

AKA

AMT.

APO

BEG

CEE

EDO

ERR

GAT

HAM

MEL

NIL

ODE

OLE ✓

PHI

SAD

SST

4 Letters

ABEL

ADEN

ALEE

ANNA

ATTY.

ELAM

ENDS

ERAS

GELS

GOES

HART

HIED

HOME

ISLE

KERR

LETT

MELD

NEED

NEWT

OGRE

OLEO

ONCE

PERU

PROS

SLUE

TELL

TOGA

YO-HO

5 Letters

ALONE

CORAL

ENTRY

ERECT

INERT

ORLON	ARLENE	OMELET
SPICY	ARTERY	PLANED
STALL	GENIAL	RASCAL
	LATENT	REAGAN
6 Letters	LAWYER	STEREO
ADMIRE	NEARER	

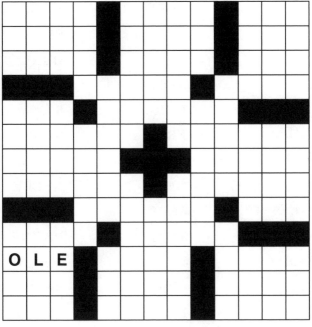

133

3 Letters

ANA
COD
FCC
GNU
HOD
ILL
INK
ION
KID
LEI
LOW
NEE
ODA
ODD
OOH
SGT.

TAX
THE
TUX
VIE

4 Letters

ACES
ACRE
ALAR ✓
ARAS
ARTY
EIRE
ERIE
FALA
GLOP
JEFF
JULY
LEAD
LEAS
LIEU

LILA
MA'AM
MEDE
MUST
ORAD
PESO
PREY
SASE
SLUR
URAL

5 Letters

AVOWS
FOODS
GELEE
PASSE
PHONE
POLED
SATYR
UPEND

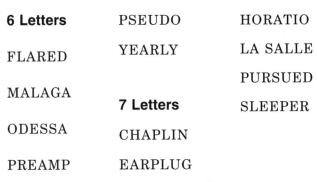

6 Letters

FLARED

MALAGA

ODESSA

PREAMP

PSEUDO

YEARLY

7 Letters

CHAPLIN

EARPLUG

HORATIO

LA SALLE

PURSUED

SLEEPER

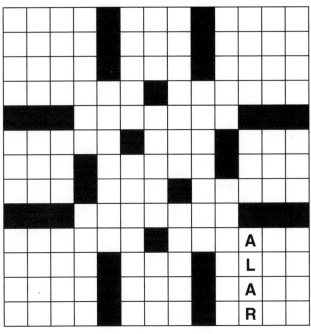

3 Letters

ADS

AIR

DAM

DNA

EBO

ENS

EOS

ERA

EYE ✓

HUH

OHM

PEA

PSI

ROM

SAC

SAM

4 Letters

A LOT

AMEN

ASHE

ASST.

DALE

DAUB

ESNE

EVIL

EYRE

HULA

IMAM

MADE

MANE

NERO

OLDS

RAGS

SARA

TIES

5 Letters

ANEAR

ANNIE

EMOTE

SIENA

STAGS

TENET

6 Letters

AERIES

ARRAYS

DANUBE

EVELYN

INDENT	VALISE	GINGERLY
LESSEE	YODELS	GLIMPSED
LLAMAS		OVERSEAS
NIELLO	**8 Letters**	SCHOONER
PONGEE	ASSEMBLY	
RAMADA	ETERNITY	

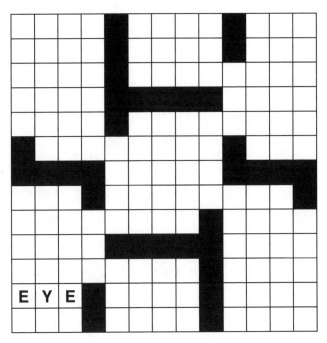

3 Letters

ALE
ANI ✓
ANT
A-OK
ELI
EVE
IOU
MAP
MAR
NAP
NOM.
NOR
SPA
TAD
VAN

WWI

4 Letters

AINU
AMAT
ANIL
ANTI
AREA
BRAD
CAPT.
CLIO
EBAN
ENOW
ERIC
IOWA
LANI
LAWN
LIST
MISO

NEVE
NOON
OLAV
PALE
PEST
SCAB
SKIP
SUNK
TERM
TICK
TURK
WINE

5 Letters

ABOUT
ALIBI
ARRAS
KRAAL
MERLE

NESTS	AU PAIR	INSERT
STRAP	BELONG	PEALED
TABLE	CABANA	RIDING
	CANADA	RITUAL
6 Letters	DIRECT	UGANDA
ADROIT	GAMINE	

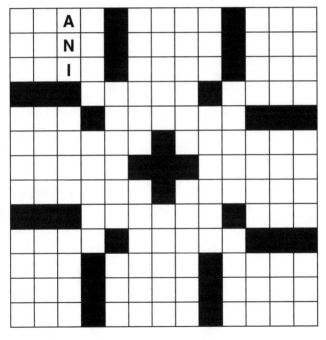

3 Letters

AWL

BBQ

BLT

BOB

EFT

ELM

FYI

ILK

KIT

LOU

NOT

RHO

RIO

RYA

SKI

SUN

TAI

TAT ✓

TBA

WHO

4 Letters

AGOG

ALLY

ALSO

BOLO

CLOG

DOOM

EGAN

EKED

ELSA

ENOL

EVEN

FATS

LOCI

NULL

OPEC

ORCA

OWED

POKY

RUNG

SNIT

SOLE

TACO

TEAM

WOVE

5 Letters

CEDAR

CLERK

LEARN

OMITS

QUASI

RABAT

SLICK

UNITY

6 Letters

DYNAST

ERASED

FELINE

O'NEILL

SPIGOT

TWIGGY

7 Letters

CAMELOT

POLYMER

REFUSAL

RESTFUL

SESSION

WACKIER

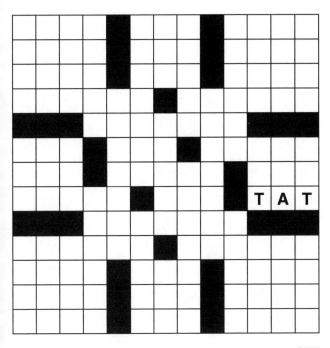

3 Letters

ALL
ALT.
BEE
CAP
DYE
EDD
IDA
KEW
LIT
LYE
ONE
PTA
RBI
TEN
TOO
TOR

UTE
YET ✓

4 Letters

ASEA
AVER
CAPO
CEDE
CHOP
CIAO
CITY
DEER
EDIE
GRAD
INDY
ITEM
KILN
LARA
LEEK
LINT

LUBE
MULL
NOAH
NORA
OWNS
SCUP
SELL
SPOT
TOED
USES
WATT
WHIG

5 Letters

CIVET
ILEUM
NOMAD
OPERA
SCALP
SWEDE

6 Letters

ALASKA

MADAME

NETTLE

OCCULT

POETIC

TAUGHT

7 Letters

ALIMONY

LIBERTY

OPTIMUM

PLATEAU

PYRAMID

WAITING

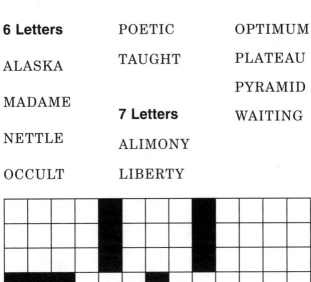

138

3 Letters

ALB
ARF
AVA
AVE.
BOO
CEO
DOT
EAU
EON
FDA
LAP
LED
LET
NBA
OUR
PEW

RAP
REE
RNA
YAW

4 Letters

AMID
ANAT.
ANNA
ANOA
BOSC
CABS
CHAR
COHO
CONE
EDGY
ERNE
HOLE
LASS
LURE

NINA
NOVA
OMAR
OVAL
RARE
SANG
SASH
SLAB ✓
STEP
TUNE

5 Letters

ARRAY
BEAST
BEECH
DECOR
EGYPT
GAYLE
OPRAH
ZONED

6 Letters

ASTRAY

CALICO

CASTOR

DRENCH

PEACHY

SWITCH

7 Letters

CLOYING

HEIGH-HO

HERETIC

PENDANT

SHATTER

WIZENED

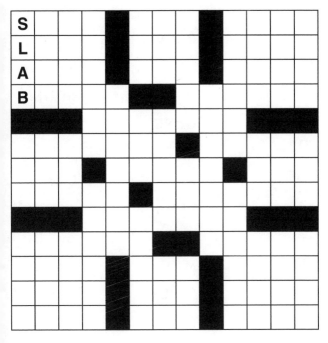

TUX

SECT

3 Letters

ARE

ATE

ATM

CUE

DEW

GNU

HIS

LOP

MAL

NAN ✓

ONO

PAL

RAH

SST

282

4 Letters

AGAR

ANNE

ARNE

AVES

CREW

DEED

EURO

GENE

GOON

KRIS

LENA

LEST

MIDI

NIBS

PACT

5 Letters

BLEEP

DACHA

EDGER

EXIST

HEEDS

HOMER

ROGER

YIELD

6 Letters

AGENCY

ANCHOR

BERATE

CANAAN

ENESCO

ERRING	RETIRE	ETHICAL
ETUDES	THANKS	HONESTY
HEARTH	TRANCE	HOUDINI
IAMBIC		MEETING
IPECAC	**7 Letters**	SPONGED
NATIVE	ANODYNE	TRIESTE

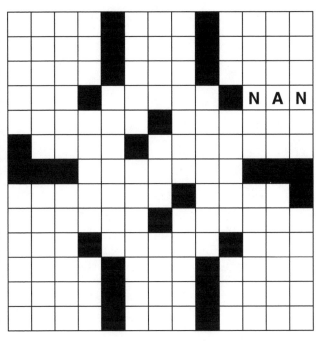

ANSWERS

1

E	R	I	C		A	F	T		B	O	A	R
T	O	R	O		D	A	Y		U	R	G	E
C	O	A	T	T	A	I	L		F	L	O	E
		O	G	R	E		F	E	N	D		
E	O	S		S	I	E	R	R	A			
C	A	T		T	O	R		E	L	I	Z	A
O	H	A	R	A		W	O	V	E	N		
L	U	R	I	D		P	R	O		A	R	E
		N	A	S	S	A	U		N	O	W	
S	L	A	G		T	E	N	N				
M	A	L	I		O	U	T	D	A	T	E	D
U	R	A	N		O	D	E		M	I	R	O
G	A	N	G		P	O	D		A	L	E	C

2

D	A	C	H	A			S	N	A	R	E
E	N	O	U	G	H		C	R	A	T	E	D
B	O	N	N	I	E		R	O	B	O	T	S
I	R	S		O	C	H	O			N	A	E
T	A	U			T	O	P	I		A	I	L
	K	L	A	X	O	N		N	U	L	L	
			A	R	R	E	S	T	S			
	H	A	H	A		S	M	O	O	T	H	
R	A	N		Y	E	T	I			E	E	L
E	N	G			M	Y	T	H		M	A	E
A	G	O	U	T	I		H	O	O	P	L	A
C	A	R	R	E	L		Y	E	L	L	E	D
T	R	A	I	T			D	E	E	D	S	

3

I	N	U	R	E			C	A	S	T	E
D	E	P	O	R	T		A	E	G	E	A	N
L	A	R	V	A	E		G	L	O	R	I	A
E	R	I	E		N	Y	E	T		A	L	T
R	E	S		O	D	I	N			P	O	E
	R	E	A	P		E	D	G	I	E	R	
			W	E	T	L	A	N	D			
	E	V	E	N	E	D		A	S	E	A	
S	E	E		L	E	E	R		T	S	P	
I	R	E		A	L	D	A		R	U	S	E
T	I	R	A	D	E		R	H	O	D	E	S
K	E	E	P	E	R		L	A	M	E	N	T
A	R	D	E	N			N	E	S	T	S	

4

G	O	A	L	I	E		S	C	O	P	E
I	N	T	A	C	T		P	E	A	L	E	D
L	E	T	T	E	R		E	A	S	I	N	G
D	R	A	T		E	E	N		H	O	N	E
	C	E	O		C	R	E	E				
N	E	H	R	U		H	O	G	W	A	S	H
I	V	E		N	E	E	D	Y		P	O	I
M	E	D	I	C	A	L		P	R	I	N	T
			N	E	R	O		T	E	A		
O	M	A	N		T	N	T		F	R	A	T
P	A	R	I	A	H		O	B	L	I	G	E
T	R	E	N	D	Y		R	E	E	S	E	S
S	T	A	G	E			S	E	X	T	E	T

286

5

K	I	N		S	C	A	N		B	L	A	T
E	D	O		A	R	N	E		I	O	N	A
G	A	R		R	O	D	E		T	R	O	N
		T	G	I	F		D	O	T	I	N	G
A	C	H	Y		T	A	F	F	Y			
T	H	E	M	E		B	U	T		R	H	O
T	A	R		N	O	B	L	E		O	E	R
U	R	N		E	K	E		N	O	S	E	D
			A	M	I	S	H		O	S	L	O
E	V	E	L	Y	N		A	S	H	E		
W	A	L	L		A	L	G	A		T	O	M
E	R	L	E		W	E	A	N		T	I	E
R	Y	A	N		A	I	R	E		I	L	L

6

P	E	R	K	Y			S	I	L	K	S	
E	L	O	I	S	E		V	I	O	L	E	T
T	E	M	P	E	R		O	R	N	A	T	E
E	V	A		R	A	N	T		M	O	E	
R	E	N	T		S	U	E		L	A	N	D
	N	O	S	I	E	R		O	I	S	E	
			K	O	R	E	A	N	S			
	L	I	E	U		Y	I	E	L	D	S	
B	O	N	D		R	E	D		E	E	L	Y
R	A	F		A	V	I	D		L	Y	E	
A	T	O	M	I	C		N	A	N	T	E	S
S	H	R	A	N	K		G	R	E	A	S	E
H	E	M	P	S			T	E	S	T	S	

7

S	W	A	M		P	A	R	E		S	U	B
L	I	D	O		A	X	I	S		C	P	A
E	N	O	W		L	E	O	P	A	R	D	S
E	G	R	E	T	S			L	E	A	H	
V	E	E	R	S			E	F	F	E	T	E
E	D	D		E	A	G	L	E		N	E	D
			T	H	O	S	E					
A	K	A		S	A	T	E	D		L	E	D
C	O	B	W	E	B			E	T	U	D	E
C	A	S	A			I	R	O	N	I	C	
E	L	E	C	T	R	I	C		T	A	S	K
D	A	N		H	O	W	E		E	C	O	L
E	S	T		Y	E	W	S		D	Y	N	E

8

I	N	T	E	R	N		S	P	E	L	L	
C	O	U	L	E	E		B	E	A	N	I	E
E	R	R	I	N	G		I	N	S	E	C	T
A	M	T		D	E	S	K		S	H	H	
G	A	L		V	O	I	D		C	E	E	
E	L	E	G	Y		U	N	I	S	O	N	
			E	A	R	N	I	N	G			
R	A	M	R	O	D		A	T	T	A	R	
L	E	S		E	V	E	R		A	V	A	
E	S	S		I	D	O	L		L	E	N	
A	C	U	M	E	N		O	O	L	O	N	G
D	U	R	I	N	G		S	P	O	N	G	E
S	E	E	D	S			T	E	N	S	E	R

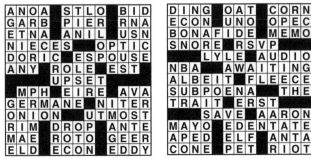

9

```
A N O A   S T L O   B I D
G A R B   P I E R   R N A
E T N A   A N I L   U S N
N I E C E S     O P T I C
D O R I C   E S P O U S E
A N Y   R O L E   E S T
        U P S E T
  M P H   E I R E   A V A
G E R M A N E   N I T E R
O N I O N   U T M O S T
R I M   D R O P   A N T E
M A E   R O T O   G E E R
E L D   E C O N   E D D Y
```

10

```
D I N G   O A T   C O R N
E C O N   U N O   O P E C
B O N A F I D E   M E M O
S N O R E   R S V P
      L Y L E   A U D I O
N B A   A W A I T I N G
A L B E I T   F L E E C E
S U B P O E N A   T H E
T R A I T   E R S T
      S A V E   A A R O N
M A Y O   E D E N T A T E
A P E D   E L F   A N T A
C O N E   P E T   R I O T
```

11

```
D O U R   B E A   S E T H
U N S E A L E D   T Y R O
G O O F B A L L   E R I N
      E E N   A L L E G E
T I E R   K R I L L
R O D   L E I   O A K E N
A N D   I T A L Y   E R A
P A Y T V   N O D   N I M
      W E L T Y   Y O K E
R E V E R E   A P E
A X E L   V A L H A L L A
K I E V   E N T I T I E S
E T R E   R A Y   S E E K
```

12

```
E R S E   M E L D   A G E
D E A N   O D O R   N O N
E L L S   N O T E   T L C
N A T U R E     W A L D O
I T E R A T E D   T E E D
C E D E D   L U C E R N E
        I C I E R
D E S M O N D   O M E G A
A N T I   N E W C O M E R
S T A G E   R E T I R E
H I T   Z O R I   E L A N
E R E   I D E S   L I L A
R E D   O A S T   S O D S
```

13

```
MOGUL   IMPOST
ORATED  REALLY
IODIDE  STREAK
   LAND COTE
SEMI  OPAH
CRUZ AWED REE
OLDEST ADJUST
TED OTIS ULNA
  SPUR KEEL
BATT  EAVE
ABOARD ROBUST
BUFFER FLORIN
STUFFY  EXIST
```

14

```
GATOR   MAPLE
ALERTS LOLLED
LINTEL OOLONG
 ENS YAWL DOE
ANY   UTAH
SASH PSI  EERY
STOA LTD EVES
TENT ORE DICE
  HOPI   DOR
EDD OPAL PER
FREEZE EMENDS
TALKED TERCET
STEED  LEERY
```

15

```
BUZZ MESS TAG
EPEE ECHO ELL
ERNE NOEL RBI
POI BULL SCAN
SATYR LAMENT
 RHEA LAZILY
  LYRICAL
 ASLEEP LENA
TRIODE EDITH
ANEW NOLA COY
BOG ETNA TEND
OLE ARCS ISAR
ODD RYES STLO
```

16

```
TARDY   CRAVE
ARARAT HEALER
DEFAME YONDER
  PSALM TOPS
SINE SINCE
TRODDEN EDICT
EMS ORSON TOO
WAHOO EXTREME
 BRIEF EROS
STOL ADOBE
TIMING RASPED
ADAGIO DREAMY
TENET  ISSUE
```

17

S	L	O	P		W	I	S	P		J	A	G
W	A	R	E		A	N	A	T		A	V	A
A	V	A	R		I	N	C	A		V	I	M
B	A	L	U	S	T	E	R		V	A	S	E
			H	E	R	E	S	Y				
H	O	T	R	O	D		D	W	I	G	H	T
A	D	I	E	U				E	N	N	U	I
T	E	M	P	L	E		L	E	G	U	M	E
			A	D	R	O	I	T				
A	C	H	Y		M	O	N	S	I	E	U	R
S	E	A		S	I	Z	E		C	U	R	E
T	I	C		O	N	E	R		O	R	A	N
I	L	K		N	E	S	S		N	O	N	O

18

H	A	G	A	R			R	E	J	E	C	T
O	L	I	V	E	R		A	R	A	B	I	A
B	Y	L	I	N	E		P	I	L	O	T	S
			S	E	M	E		C	O	N	E	S
A	G	L	O	W		S	W	A	P			
E	L	I			A	N	T	A		Y	A	R	N
R	I	M		L	A	R	R	Y		L	A	Y
O	B	E	Y		T	A	P	E		A	M	P
			A	P	O	D		A	H	E	A	D
S	H	A	M	E		A	G	R	A			
N	O	R	M	A	N		E	E	R	I	E	R
A	P	I	E	C	E		E	N	T	R	E	E
G	E	A	R	E	D			D	E	A	N	S

19

S	S	T		T	R	E	T		E	G	A	D
U	R	N		Y	O	Y	O		M	I	S	O
M	O	T	O	R	M	E	N		B	L	E	W
			B	O	A		T	A	R	T	A	N
S	O	S	O		I	R	O	N	Y			
A	N	T	E	N	N	A		I	O	N	I	A
N	Y	E		Y	E	S	E	S		O	T	T
E	X	P	E	L		P	R	E	F	E	C	T
			T	O	K	Y	O		A	S	H	Y
V	I	C	U	N	A		S	O	W			
E	N	I	D		P	O	I	G	N	A	N	T
A	R	N	E		O	D	O	R		M	O	I
L	E	E	S		K	A	N	E		A	W	L

20

D	U	S	K		I	V	Y		S	A	G	S
O	N	T	O		M	A	E		C	L	A	N
D	E	A	R		O	I	L		R	A	R	E
D	A	N	E		G	N	P		E	S	T	E
E	S	C	A	P	E		S	H	A	K	E	R
R	E	E		I	N	C		O	M	A	R	
			N	E	P	A	L					
	P	U	T	T		A	G	E		C	A	D
H	A	N	S	O	M		I	D	E	A	T	E
A	S	H	E		A	R	T		A	N	T	E
S	C	O	T		T	E	A		M	A	A	M
T	A	O	S		T	A	T		E	D	I	E
E	L	K	E		E	R	E		S	A	N	D

21

```
O S C A R   A C R E S
C H A L E T   O R I E N T
T A R T A R   A M A N D A
E R R   M Y T H   T U T
T K O   I O U   Y A R E
  S T R O N G   R O L E
    H A G G L E D
  A L E F   E L P A S O
F L E A   E R A   O R E
A K A   G Y M S   L A D
C A S A B A   A I L I N G
E L E V E N   S L E D G E
R I S E N   L O S E R
```

22

```
C A M E O   R U L E D
O D E S S A   P E S E T A
M A N T I S   A C C O R D
E M U   R H I N E   N E E
    T I T L E D
P A R A S O L   E L A N D
A M E R   N B A   A N O A
L I O N S   R U S H I N G
    K E E P E R
B O N   A D D A X   E A R
A G O U T I   I T H A C A
S E S T E T   R E E V E S
K E Y E D   T W E R P
```

23

```
I S A I A H   S H E L F
B O G G L E   S H A V E R
E L I N O R   E R R A T A
X E N O N   S N I P
    B E R T   F O U N T
S E L L   O U S T   R O O
A L E E   U N O   A G O G
U S A   G E N U   L E N O
L E H A R   E P I C
    P A I R   N O T E D
C I T R I C   A D H E R E
U R S I N E   D I O N N E
R E P L Y   S A L T E D
```

24

```
T A M E D   P A G I N G
A N I M A L   A R A B I A
R E L I V E   P O S I N G
O M E L E T   M O D E S
  O P E   T O R A H
O N O   R I S O T T O
N E S T   A G O   L O R E
E S T R A D A   O A R
    I R E N E   M T V
B R I B E   D I E S E L
L A G U N A   A T T I R E
A T O N A L   M E R E S T
H E R E S Y   M O S E S
```

27   **28**

29

```
J A R   H A S T   L I D O
A G O   O R C A   A R A B
W E D G W O O D   H A L O
      E L M O   E R N I E
L E A N   A T O M
O W L E T     A M P E R E
W E A V E R   R E A R E D
E R R A T A     T R I B E
      R Y A N   D E A N
M O O L A   P O C O
O K L A   A R R A N G E D
O R A N   S I M P   A T E
N A V E   P L A T   G A B
```

30

```
P U L L   H E N   F A L A
A R I A   I R A   R E E L
L A N I   P E C T O R A L
E N A C T S   R O M A N O
R I G   U T T E R   T E T
  C E N T E R   B E D S
      A U R I C L E
J U T E   C R A G G Y
A P O   G R E A T   L O T
S T U D I O   D E F I N E
P A R A L L E L   E D D A
E K E D   E V E   T E E M
R E D S   S A D   E R R S
```

31

```
E D N A   A R C   N A P A
D E E M   B A H   E P O S
G A V E   E M U   H I N T
A L A R M   G A R A G E
R E D I A L   S U R E R
  R A C C O O N S   Y E N
      A R D U O U S
A S K   A I R D R O M E
S T E A M   S E D A N S
H E E D E D   S A L S A
R E P O   U K E   P A U L
A V E R   L A W   O G E E
M E R E   L Y E   P A S S
```

32

```
C A N A A N   C R A Z E
I B E R I A   H E E L E D
N E A T L Y   A L L I E D
E L L E     F L O
    R E A C T   A S A P
L A N Y A R D   A D E L A
O B I   R E R U N   M E T
T U L I P   O S T R I C H
S T E P   S M A S H
      E K E     O V E R
B O C C I E   M A N I L A
U N H A N D   O L D E S T
D E I C E   T E A S E S
```

33

E	L	M		J	O	K	E		A	R	N	O
L	I	T		A	M	E	N		D	O	O	R
L	E	V	E	R	A	G	E		D	O	N	A
			A	S	H		M	O	L	D	E	D
F	O	P	S		A	G	I	L	E			
E	T	H	Y	L		L	E	S	S	O	N	S
U	T	E		E	R	O	S	E		N	E	O
D	O	W	A	G	E	R		N	I	T	R	O
			V	I	N	Y	L		N	O	O	N
C	A	P	O	T	E		L	U	G			
E	N	O	W		W	E	A	K	E	N	E	D
O	I	S	E		A	R	N	E		B	E	A
S	L	E	D		L	A	O	S		C	N	N

34

E	R	N	E		W	I	M	P		L	A	B
N	E	A	R		I	D	O	L		O	D	E
A	S	P	S		N	A	T	O		G	A	R
M	A	K	E	R	S		T	W	I	G	G	Y
E	L	I		O	L	E	O		V	E	I	L
L	E	N		B	O	W		A	E	R	O	
			O	W	I	N	G					
W	A	T	T		N	A	G		P	B	S	
G	E	N	U		A	G	N	I		O	R	O
R	A	G	T	A	G		N	E	T	T	E	D
I	K	E		W	A	D	I		A	P	E	D
M	E	L		E	P	E	E		S	I	Z	E
E	N	S		S	E	W	S		K	E	E	N

35

O	V	E	N		R	A	E		P	A	L	E
M	I	N	I		O	P	T		E	R	I	N
A	V	O	N		S	E	A		S	E	E	D
R	A	W	E	S	T		P	A	E	A	N	S
			U	R	G	E	N	T				
T	I	E		B	U	R		O	A	T	E	R
O	R	T		S	M	E	L	T		E	G	O
O	K	A	P	I		B	A	H		A	G	E
			A	D	H	E	R	E				
E	M	B	R	Y	O		G	R	I	P	E	D
B	A	R	I		G	E	E		N	A	P	E
A	X	I	S		A	B	S		G	L	E	N
N	I	G	H		N	O	T		A	M	E	S

36

L	A	P	P		C	U	P	S		M	O	D
O	A	H	U		I	N	R	E		A	C	E
D	R	O	P		A	W	E	D		R	E	P
G	O	T		P	O	I	S	E		T	A	I
E	N	O	L	A		S	I	R		I	N	C
			O	I	L	E	D		K	N	I	T
	D	O	W	R	Y		I	O	N	I	C	
P	E	R	E		R	H	O	N	E			
A	N	D		R	I	O		C	E	L	L	O
R	E	E		E	C	O	L	E		A	L	P
C	U	R		V	I	V	A		S	T	A	T
E	V	E		U	S	E	D		A	C	M	E
L	E	D		E	T	R	E		C	H	A	D

37

M	U	D		A	C	R	E		A	B	B	A
E	R	E		W	H	E	T		C	U	L	T
M	A	L		L	A	T	E		E	S	T	E
O	L	I	O		F	A	R	M	S			
			D	E	F	I	N	E		A	H	A
A	R	B	O	R		N	A	T		L	A	C
H	U	R	R	A	H		L	E	V	A	N	T
E	D	O		S	E	A		O	I	N	K	S
M	E	W		E	L	T	O	R	O			
			E	D	I	T	S		L	A	K	E
O	L	A	V		P	E	A	L		L	I	L
R	I	G	A		A	N	K	A		O	W	L
E	D	E	N		D	D	A	Y		T	I	S

38

O	W	N	E	R			G	E	S	T	E	
S	H	I	V	E	R		G	A	M	I	E	R
C	A	N	A	D	A		A	L	U	M	N	A
A	L	E			C	E	L	L		I	T	S
R	E	T		G	Y	R	O			L	E	E
	R	Y	A	N		E	R	O	D	E	D	
			L	A	R	C	E	N	Y			
	N	I	T	W	I	T		L	E	N	O	
S	E	N		D	E	W	Y		O	R	T	
W	A	C		E	D	D	A			T	A	R
A	T	O	N	A	L		D	E	B	A	T	E
R	E	M	O	T	E		E	L	A	T	E	S
D	R	E	G	S				D	R	E	S	S

39

M	I	L	A	N			A	N	O	D	E	S
A	B	I	D	E	D		R	A	W	E	S	T
L	E	N	D	E	R		E	N	E	S	C	O
I	R	E		D	A	P		A	D	O	R	N
C	I	A		I	M	A	M			T	O	Y
E	A	R	L	E		T	A	L	L	O	W	
		A	S	H	T	R	A	Y				
	H	O	G	T	I	E		N	E	P	A	L
B	E	Y		T	R	O	D		E	B	O	
L	A	S	S	O		N	I	L		T	A	W
A	L	T	A	R	S		S	A	L	U	T	E
S	T	E	R	E	O		E	D	I	L	E	S
T	H	R	A	L	L			Y	E	A	S	T

40

B	E	N		A	M	I	D		D	E	M	O
O	B	I		P	O	N	E		O	D	I	N
S	O	N	A	T	I	N	A		R	O	L	E
S	N	A	G			L	L	A	M	A	S	
			O	M	I	T	T	E	D			
E	N	S	N	A	R	E		T	O	R	C	H
F	O	E		S	K	E	E	T		E	A	U
T	R	E	A	T		T	W	E	L	F	T	H
			F	I	S	H	E	R	Y			
S	C	A	R	C	E			R	A	S	H	
O	L	G	A		V	I	O	L	E	N	C	E
R	A	N	I		E	R	L	E		T	A	M
E	N	I	D		N	A	D	A		I	N	S

41

B	E	T		A	N	T	A		V	A	M	P
R	N	A		M	A	A	M		I	D	O	L
I	R	S		I	N	T	O		D	O	N	A
D	A	T	E	D			K	E	E	N	A	N
A	G	E	L	E	S	S		V	O	I	C	E
L	E	D	A		P	O	S	E		S	O	D
			M	E	R	C	U	R	Y			
A	S	P		T	Y	K	E		S	E	E	M
C	H	I	N	A		O	T	H	E	L	L	O
R	E	S	E	L	L			A	R	M	E	D
O	R	T	S		A	D	D	S		I	V	E
S	P	O	T		S	U	I	T		R	E	S
S	A	N	S		H	O	N	E		A	N	T

42

T	H	R	A	C	E		S	P	O	R	E
Y	O	U	T	H	S		P	I	L	A	T	E
R	A	S	H	E	S		G	R	E	T	E	L
E	R	S	E		C	A	S	A				
			N	O	E	L			S	W	A	B
E	N	L	A	R	G	E		H	E	A	V	E
N	E	E		A	G	A	T	E		D	O	R
D	I	V	A	N		N	U	R	S	I	N	G
S	L	I	P		E	B	A	N				
			P	O	U	R			O	N	T	O
S	W	E	A	R	S		S	H	O	O	I	N
P	O	L	L	E	N		R	E	Z	O	N	E
Y	E	L	L	S			O	P	E	N	E	R

43

S	K	I		E	R	A	S		S	I	Z	E
A	R	M		L	A	N	A		I	T	E	M
L	A	P		O	M	A	R		T	H	A	I
A	M	A		P	A	T	I	O		A	L	L
M	E	L	E	E			D	E	C	O	Y	
I	R	A	Q		A	U	T	O	M	A	T	
			U	N	I	F	O	R	M			
	T	R	A	I	T	O	R		E	A	V	E
K	R	I	L	L			S	T	E	I	N	
N	I	P		E	V	E	R	Y		R	O	C
O	V	E	R		A	C	E	R		A	L	I
W	I	S	H		L	O	D	I		T	E	N
N	A	T	O		E	L	S	A		E	T	A

44

M	O	P		S	T	E	P		P	A	S	S
A	C	E		C	O	D	A		O	S	L	O
N	C	O		A	T	O	N		O	L	E	O
T	U	R	T	L	E		E	I	L	E	E	N
I	L	I	A	D		A	L	F		E	V	E
S	T	A	B		L	E	I	F		P	E	R
			C	O	R	N	Y					
A	D	S		H	A	I	G		U	S	M	C
L	E	N		U	T	E		S	P	E	A	R
A	W	E	I	G	H		I	C	I	C	L	E
S	L	E	D		I	N	G	E		T	O	W
K	A	R	L		N	E	O	N		O	N	E
A	P	S	E		G	O	R	E		R	E	D

45

P	O	S	Y		C	A	D		H	O	L	D
O	G	E	E		A	V	A		A	P	I	A
E	R	A	L		R	E	V	E	R	E	N	D
T	E	M	P	L	E		E	N	T	R	E	E
			E	Y	E	R		G	E	E		
G	A	R	D	E	N	I	A		T	E	A	
E	K	E		S	E	C	C	O		T	E	D
M	A	E		D	E	C	K	H	A	N	D	
	N	B	C		R	E	L	Y				
A	S	T	R	A	Y		N	A	M	I	N	G
C	H	E	A	P	E	S	T		N	O	U	N
H	E	R	D		W	E	E		A	N	N	A
E	A	S	Y		S	A	D		L	A	S	T

46

F	E	T	E		M	I	L	A		T	E	T
A	M	I	D		A	R	A	L		U	S	O
N	I	N	E		D	A	D	O		R	P	M
G	L	A	N	C	E		L	E	O	N		
			R	I	D	E		W	O	R	E	
B	I	T		E	R	R		S	E	V	E	N
A	S	H		T	A	U	N	T		E	B	O
A	L	A	T	E		N	A	E		R	A	W
L	E	N	A		A	K	I	N				
	K	I	E	V		V	O	L	L	E	Y
R	A	F		S	I	T	E		E	U	R	O
E	M	U		P	S	S	T		E	R	I	K
M	I	L		Y	O	K	E		R	E	N	O

47

P	U	R	R		E	O	N		G	R	O	G
A	N	O	A		R	B	I		R	O	T	O
N	I	T	R	O	G	E	N		O	T	T	O
S	T	E	E	P		Y	O	H	O			
			F	U	N		N	O	V	E	N	A
B	A	B	Y	L	O	N		M	E	T	A	L
A	G	O		E	T	U	D	E		C	P	A
L	I	N	E	N		B	U	T	C	H	E	R
I	N	D	U	C	T		O	O	H			
			C	E	O	S		W	A	D	E	D
A	M	A	H		Q	U	A	N	T	I	T	Y
N	O	I	R		U	R	N		T	A	R	E
N	O	D	E		E	F	T		Y	S	E	R

48

A	I	D	E		A	W	E	S		C	U	R
C	R	E	W		S	H	A	G		A	N	Y
T	O	N	E		P	O	R	T		N	E	D
O	N	O		S	A	L		D	O	V	E	
R	E	T	R	O		D	E	A	L	E	R	
	D	E	E	D		D	O	L	M	A	N	
		P	D	J	A	M	E	S				
	P	U	L	L	E	D		M	E	R	V	
P	A	P	A	Y	A		I	L	E	U	M	
I	N	K	Y		L	A	Y		A	L	E	
N	E	E		F	O	R	E		O	R	C	A
O	L	E		D	U	E	L		P	E	A	R
T	S	P		A	S	A	P		E	D	N	A

49

A	D	O	B	E			C	R	U	S	T	Y
R	E	P	O	R	T		H	O	N	C	H	O
E	L	I	X	I	R		A	B	O	A	R	D
N	U	N		E	O	N	S			M	O	E
A	D	E	S		P	O	M	E		P	A	L
	E	S	P	R	I	T		A	L	I	T	
		R	E	C	E	I	V	E				
	M	A	Y	A		P	O	E	T	R	Y	
S	I	C		R	O	A	D		T	E	E	D
P	R	O		A	D	I	T		F	L	Y	
L	A	R	G	E	R		N	O	D	U	L	E
I	G	N	O	R	E		E	R	A	S	E	R
T	E	S	T	E	D			S	L	E	D	S

50

F	E	A	S	T			T	A	P	E	R	S
A	D	R	O	I	T		O	M	E	L	E	T
T	I	L	L	E	R		W	A	P	I	T	I
A	T	E		A	P	E			N	I	L	
L	O	N		E	V	E	R	T		O	R	T
	R	E	E	L	E	D		W	I	R	E	
		B	A	L	D	W	I	N				
	D	E	B	T		L	A	S	S	E	S	
L	I	E		E	X	E	R	T		C	E	E
I	V	Y			E	D	D			L	A	B
V	I	O	L	I	N		E	L	P	A	S	O
E	N	R	I	C	O		N	O	T	I	O	N
D	E	E	P	E	N			B	A	R	N	S

51

J	U	G		S	C	A	R		R	A	G	A
U	P	I		H	I	R	E		I	V	A	N
N	O	D		E	P	I	C		G	A	L	A
K	N	E	W		H	A	I	F	A			
			A	D	E	S	T	E		T	B	A
M	A	T	H	E	R		E	E	R	I	E	R
A	L	O	O	F				B	E	R	E	T
R	E	L	O	A	D		S	L	E	E	P	Y
T	E	D		M	E	L	T	E	D			
			L	E	M	U	R		Y	O	W	L
B	A	B	Y		U	R	A	L		A	W	E
A	M	E	N		R	A	F	T		S	I	T
A	P	E	X		E	Y	E	D		T	I	S

52

B	O	L	T		M	I	N		R	O	A	M
A	L	A	E		O	N	E		Y	U	M	A
A	G	H	A		A	T	H	L	E	T	I	C
L	A	R	K			E	R	A				
			W	A	L	R	U	S		U	S	S
B	E	D	O	U	I	N		A	K	R	O	N
E	X	H	O	R	T		A	G	E	N	D	A
S	P	O	D	E		W	I	N	E	S	A	P
T	O	W		A	N	I	M	A	L			
			T	I	C				B	R	A	N
H	E	N	P	E	C	K	S		O	A	H	U
A	L	B	A		H	E	R		A	M	A	T
P	L	A	Y		E	D	O		T	A	B	S

53

S	O	B	B	E	D		E	D	G	E	S
T	R	O	I	K	A		D	E	A	R	T	H
A	D	O	B	E	S		U	N	L	A	C	E
R	E	T		H	O	P		C	H	E		
T	A	I		R	I	C	E		D	I	E	T
	L	E	V	A	N	T		R	E	D	S	
		E	N	G	O	R	G	E				
A	F	A	R		B	E	A	G	L	E		
B	E	S	T		P	E	S	T		I	R	S
B	A	T		S	R	O		M	A	E		
E	L	E	C	T	S		U	P	R	I	S	E
S	T	R	E	E	T		N	E	T	T	E	D
S	Y	N	O	D		D	R	E	S	S	Y	

54

A	R	G	U	E		F	R	A	I	L
B	O	U	N	C	E		F	I	E	S	T	A
C	E	N	S	O	R		O	R	A	T	E	D
			O	N	E	A	L		D	A	R	E
F	R	A	U		W	I	F	E				
E	A	R	N		B	E	A	U		E	E	K
A	G	A	D	I	R		G	R	E	A	S	E
R	E	B		K	I	N	E		X	R	A	Y
			Y	E	T	I		P	L	U	S	
A	L	A	E		A	X	I	A	L			
S	O	M	A	L	I		W	R	A	S	S	E
A	R	I	S	E	N		W	E	I	G	H	S
P	I	E	T	A			A	N	T	E	S	

55

M	A	S	H	E	D		S	A	B	I	N
E	N	T	I	R	E		S	L	E	E	V	E
E	N	E	R	G	Y		P	A	N	T	E	D
K	A	T	E			E	W	E				
			D	R	E	A	D		A	B	B	A
A	H	S		U	R	N		U	S	U	R	P
B	A	H		D	R	O	L	L		R	A	E
B	R	O	A	D		D	O	N		L	E	D
E	D	O	M		G	E	T	A	T			
			B	O	A			E	A	S	Y	
V	I	O	L	I	N		P	R	E	S	T	O
E	L	D	E	S	T		B	O	T	H	E	R
G	L	A	D	E		S	C	H	E	M	E	

56

S	L	O	S	H		A	S	H	E	R
K	O	R	E	A	N		E	L	T	O	R	O
E	S	T	A	T	E		L	E	A	R	N	S
W	E	S	T		A	I	M		N	A	E	S
			E	M	P	T	I	E	D			
S	P	O	D	E		E	R	A	S	I	N	G
U	F	O		A	U	R	A	S		D	E	E
E	C	H	I	D	N	A		E	N	A	T	E
			R	E	S	T	Y	L	E			
A	R	G	O		N	E	E		L	A	V	E
V	I	E	N	N	A		L	E	S	S	E	N
A	S	L	E	E	P		L	O	O	T	E	D
R	E	T	R	O			S	N	I	P	S	

57

R	E	T	I	A			S	A	M	O	S
I	C	A	R	U	S		D	I	V	E	R	T
O	R	N	E	R	Y		U	G	A	N	D	A
T	U	G		O	R	G	A	N		D	O	G
			C	R	U	L	L	E	R			
R	E	S	H	A	P	E		D	U	E	L	S
C	L	E	O		Y	E	T		M	A	Y	O
A	D	E	P	T		F	A	V	O	R	E	D
		S	E	C	U	L	A	R				
R	O	T		F	O	L	K	S		C	B	S
O	R	I	E	L	S		E	S	C	O	R	T
B	A	L	B	O	A		D	A	H	L	I	A
E	L	T	O	N			L	I	T	E	R	

58

E	N	T	R	Y			C	L	E	A	V	E
P	U	R	E	E		C	R	A	M	P	E	D
S	T	E	E	L		R	E	B	U	I	L	D
O	R	B		P	R	O	D			E	L	I
M	I	L	D		I	C	O	N		C	U	E
	A	E	R	A	T	E		A	H	E	M	
			A	G	E		E	V	A			
	F	E	T	A		T	R	Y	I	N	G	
A	I	L		R	A	Y	S		G	A	L	L
B	A	D			S	P	E	W		M	A	L
A	N	E	M	O	N	E		A	M	I	N	O
S	C	R	A	P	E	D		N	A	N	C	Y
H	E	S	T	E	R			E	D	G	E	D

59

D	E	B	A	T	E			B	E	L	I	E
A	T	O	N	E	D		V	E	N	I	C	E
D	A	R	T	E	D		C	R	A	T	E	R
O	L	E	I	N			R	E	M	E	D	Y
			Y	E	W		F	O	R			
A	U	R	A		R	E	S	T	R	A	I	N
S	P	I	N		I	L	K		E	T	N	A
P	I	N	N	A	C	L	E		D	I	C	E
		G	O	B		S	P	Y				
D	E	L	T	A	S			A	S	C	O	T
O	L	E	A	T	E		S	H	E	E	N	A
M	I	T	T	E	N		S	O	A	R	E	D
E	A	S	E	D			T	O	N	E	R	S

60

S	C	A	R	C	E			L	E	M	O	N
H	O	M	E	R	S		T	U	X	E	D	O
I	M	A	G	E	S		H	A	U	L	E	D
N	O	T	E	D			O	U	R			
			N	I	C	E	R		B	E	R	G
S	P	E	C	T	E	R			T	O	O	
T	I	D	Y		O	R	T		O	U	T	S
A	N	D			O	S	T	R	I	C	H	
B	E	Y	S		I	R	K	E	D			
		W	I	N			R	E	R	A	N	
R	A	T	I	N	G		S	C	R	A	P	E
O	R	A	N	G	E		R	E	E	V	E	S
M	E	D	E	A			O	L	D	E	S	T

300

61

O	R	E	L		S	P	U	N		F	C	C
L	U	T	E		Y	A	R	E		A	H	A
D	E	A	N		N	E	N	E		S	I	S
		I	N	C	A		D	U	T	C	H	
L	L	A	N	O		N	A	Y	S			
O	E	R		M	A	S	K		E	L	S	E
A	N	T	H	E	M		I	N	D	E	N	T
M	A	Y	A		M	A	N	O		A	I	R
			R	O	O	F		T	O	R	T	E
C	R	E	P	T		L	I	E	U			
L	A	M		H	O	O	D		T	B	A	R
A	T	M		E	R	A	L		D	E	B	T
P	E	A		R	O	T	E		O	N	C	E

62

T	A	R	A		S	A	N		K	I	L	T
I	B	I	D		T	H	E		I	S	A	R
L	E	B	A	N	E	S	E		B	E	D	E
			G	Y	M		D	R	I	E	S	T
A	R	N	I	E		F	I	A	T			
S	H	O	O		F	R	E	N	Z	I	E	D
P	E	G		B	R	I	S	K		T	I	E
S	A	S	S	I	E	S	T		T	E	R	M
			T	R	E	K		T	I	M	E	S
R	I	Y	A	D	H		N	A	G			
E	D	O	M		A	M	E	T	H	Y	S	T
B	O	D	E		N	B	A		T	E	E	S
A	L	A	N		D	A	P		S	N	A	P

63

I	N	P	U	T			A	K	I	M	B	O
N	E	L	S	O	N		R	E	L	I	E	D
C	R	A	N	N	Y		M	E	L	D	E	D
H	O	T		G	E	T	O	N		I	T	S
		L	A	T	E	R	A	L				
A	I	D	A		L	E	N	I	E	N	T	
W	O	O	D		D	A	D		T	R	U	E
	N	U	R	E	Y	E	V		H	A	N	D
			N	O	M	I	N	E	E			
C	A	P		N	E	V	I	L		A	A	H
U	G	A	N	D	A		N	U	A	N	C	E
E	I	L	E	E	N		E	D	I	T	E	D
S	N	E	E	R	S			E	M	E	R	Y

64

M	A	Y	O		S	O	L		S	P	A	S
I	G	O	R		A	W	E		H	U	L	L
S	I	K	A		T	L	C		E	L	S	A
T	O	O	T	H	Y		T	A	L	L	O	W
			O	U	R	S	E	L	F			
B	L	U	R	B		U	R	I		I	V	E
Y	E	T		B	E	I	N	G		O	I	L
E	W	E		A	L	T		H	O	N	E	Y
			C	R	U	E	L	T	Y			
A	P	H	I	D	S		I	S	S	U	E	S
D	R	E	G		I	R	K		T	R	O	T
D	O	R	A		V	E	E		E	D	N	A
S	P	A	R		E	O	S		R	U	S	T

65

I	S	N	T		B	L	T		O	V	A	L
S	H	E	A		R	O	W		N	I	C	E
L	A	W	N		O	B	I		O	R	C	A
A	V	E		P	A	S	S	E		G	O	P
M	E	S	H	E	D		T	S	H	I	R	T
	S	T	A	T	E	D		S	O	L	D	
			R	U	N	O	V	E	R			
	L	I	E	N		M	I	N	D	E	D	
H	E	R	M	I	T		O	C	E	L	O	T
E	D	O		A	I	S	L	E		U	N	O
A	G	N	I		A	M	A		A	D	A	R
V	E	E	R		R	O	T		G	E	L	S
E	R	R	S		A	G	E		O	R	D	O

66

K	A	R	L		S	H	H		A	B	E	L
O	G	E	E		C	E	O		V	E	A	L
K	A	N	E		R	P	M		E	R	G	O
O	D	E	S	S	A		E	E	R	I	L	Y
M	I	G		E	W	E	R	S		N	E	D
O	R	E	G	A	N	O		T	O	G	S	
			E	L	Y	S	I	A	N			
	A	R	E	A		I	N	T	E	R	I	M
P	G	A		N	O	N	C	E		E	B	O
L	E	N	G	T	H		E	S	P	I	E	D
I	N	G	E		A	N	N		I	N	R	E
E	D	E	N		R	E	S		N	E	I	L
D	A	R	T		A	T	E		E	R	A	S

67

J	A	S	P	E	R			S	T	A	N	D
U	P	T	A	K	E		S	E	R	V	E	R
D	I	A	D	E	M		O	N	I	O	N	Y
Y	A	R	D		N	I	P		O	W	E	S
			L	E	A	S	H	E	D			
I	N	F	E	R	N	O		G	E	S	T	E
M	O	B		O	T	T	E	R		P	A	R
P	R	I	E	D		O	P	E	N	A	I	R
			R	E	U	N	I	T	E			
A	D	A	M		L	E	T		E	L	L	A
R	E	G	I	O	N		O	R	D	E	A	L
A	M	A	N	D	A		M	A	L	O	N	E
B	O	R	E	D			E	D	E	N	I	C

68

K	I	E	L		S	R	O		S	L	O	E
I	S	L	E		P	E	N		T	O	L	L
D	E	A	R		E	V	E		U	R	A	L
D	E	M	O	T	E		A	R	R	I	V	E
			Y	O	D	E	L	E	D			
B	O	G		P	E	P		C	Y	N	I	C
U	R	N		I	R	O	N	Y		B	A	A
G	O	U	D	A		D	O	C		C	N	N
			O	R	D	E	R	L	Y			
E	M	B	R	Y	O		F	E	E	L	E	R
R	O	A	M		N	C	O		A	U	R	A
A	P	S	E		E	E	L		S	C	O	T
L	E	E	R		E	E	K		T	E	S	S

69

70

71

72

73

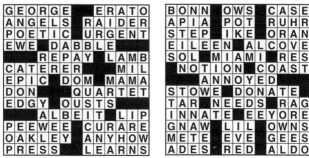

G	E	O	R	G	E				E	R	A	T	O
A	N	G	E	L	S		R	A	I	D	E	R	
P	O	E	T	I	C		U	R	G	E	N	T	
E	W	E			D	A	B	B	L	E			
			R	E	P	A	Y			L	A	M	B
C	A	T	E	R	E	R					M	I	L
E	P	I	C			D	O	M		M	A	M	A
D	O	N				Q	U	A	R	T	E	T	
E	D	G	Y		O	U	S	T	S				
			A	L	B	E	I	T			L	I	P
P	E	E	W	E	E		C	U	R	A	R	E	
O	A	K	L	E	Y		A	N	Y	H	O	W	
P	R	E	S	S			L	E	A	R	N	S	

74

B	O	N	N		O	W	S		C	A	S	E	
A	P	I	A		P	O	T		R	U	H	R	
S	T	E	P		I	K	E		O	R	A	N	
E	I	L	E	E	N		A	L	C	O	V	E	
S	O	L		M	I	A	M	I		R	E	S	
	N	O	T	I	O	N		C	O	A	S	T	
			A	N	N	O	Y	E	D				
S	T	O	W	E		D	O	N	A	T	E		
T	A	R		N	E	E	D	S		R	A	G	
I	N	N	A	T	E		E	E	Y	O	R	E	
G	N	A	W		L	I	L		O	W	N	S	
M	E	T	E		E	V	E		G	E	E	S	
A	D	E	S		R	E	D		A	L	D	O	

75

S	A	L	I	N	A			A	B	E	L	E	
C	R	A	N	E	S		S	L	A	T	E	D	
U	N	W	R	A	P		L	A	N	C	E	D	
D	O	N	O	R		T	I	N	T				
			A	E	S	O	P			U	S	E	S
G	U	M	D	R	O	P				O	L	E	
A	R	A	S		Y	I	P		L	A	K	E	
V	A	N			C	A	L	I	P	E	R		
E	L	S	A		B	A	T	I	K				
			S	E	L	L		T	A	C	I	T	
F	A	R	I	N	A		E	M	B	O	D	Y	
R	I	Y	A	D	H		F	U	L	L	E	R	
O	M	E	N	S			T	S	E	T	S	E	

76

G	O	N	G		S	P	A		S	C	A	B	
O	P	A	L		L	A	W		H	O	R	A	
R	I	T	A		U	S	A		E	A	R	N	
E	N	A	M	O	R		K	L	A	X	O	N	
S	E	N	O	R		V	E	E		E	Y	E	
	S	T	U	D		I	N	C		D	O	R	
			R	I	P	O	S	T	E				
I	C	E		N	I	L		U	C	L	A		
M	O	M		A	V	A		R	O	O	T	S	
P	U	E	B	L	O		R	E	L	A	T	E	
A	G	R	A		T	A	O		O	V	I	D	
R	A	G	S		A	C	T		G	E	R	E	
T	R	E	K		L	E	A		Y	S	E	R	

77

P	E	L	E	E				O	S	C	A	R
A	B	I	D	E	D		S	A	T	I	R	E
G	A	M	I	N	E		P	R	E	A	M	P
E	N	O	L		L	A	C		R	O	S	S
			E	L	E	V	A	T	E			
P	U	L	S	A	T	E		H	O	M	E	R
A	N	I		D	E	N	S	E		B	O	A
M	O	T	E	L		G	E	R	M	A	N	E
		R	E	F	E	R	E	E				
A	G	A	R		A	R	E		N	A	N	A
L	A	R	I	A	T		N	I	A	C	I	N
T	R	E	N	T	E		E	N	C	I	N	O
O	S	A	G	E				S	E	D	A	N

78

F	L	O	E		P	S	I		S	H	O	W
R	E	F	R	A	I	N	S		T	A	R	A
I	N	F	E	R	N	A	L		A	R	A	L
E	D	I	C	T		P	A	D	L	O	C	K
S	E	C	T				N	I	E	L	L	O
	R	E	E	K		A	D	D		D	E	N
			D	E	B	U	S	S	Y			
A	B	S		Y	A	K		T	A	T	S	
R	A	C	K	E	T			W	R	A	P	
B	L	O	N	D	I	E		E	N	A	T	E
O	B	O	E		S	T	R	A	I	N	E	R
R	O	P	E		T	R	O	U	N	C	E	S
S	A	S	S		E	E	N		G	E	N	E

79

P	O	M	P		D	O	R		A	D	A	M
L	U	A	U		I	D	A		L	E	V	I
A	S	S	T		O	A	T		A	B	E	T
N	E	T	T	E	D		A	L	M	O	S	T
			E	X	E	R	T	I	O	N		
T	W	E	R	P		H	A	N		A	S	H
B	A	D		O	M	I	T	S		I	O	U
A	N	I		S	O	N		E	A	R	L	E
		T	E	E	T	E	R	E	D			
H	A	I	R	D	O		O	D	D	J	O	B
A	N	O	A		R	O	M		L	A	V	A
H	I	N	T		E	T	A		E	D	E	N
A	L	S	O		D	O	N		D	E	N	S

80

D	I	L	L	O	N		E	R	R	A	T	A
O	N	E	I	D	A		F	E	E	L	E	R
G	N	O	M	E	S		T	A	L	E	N	T
			E	S	T			L	A	S	T	S
G	L	A	D		Y	U	M	M	Y			
O	A	R			N	O	S	E	B	A	G	
B	R	A	M		F	L	O		D	I	D	O
S	A	M	U	R	A	I			T	A	B	
		S	I	X	T	Y		S	E	M	I	
M	A	R	I	A			E	K	E			
O	R	A	C	L	E		A	L	C	O	V	E
P	I	N	A	T	A		R	E	T	A	I	L
S	A	I	L	O	R		N	E	S	T	E	D

81

S	C	A	D		R	E	M		B	Y	T	E
T	A	P	A		O	L	E		O	V	I	D
A	S	S	I	G	N	E	D		R	E	E	D
G	E	E	S	E		V	A	N	E	S	S	A
			Y	O	D	E	L	E	D			
R	U	T		R	U	N		W	O	V	E	N
T	R	U	D	G	E		A	D	M	I	R	E
E	N	N	U	I		A	L	E		A	G	E
			C	A	S	T	I	L	E			
F	I	S	H	N	E	T		H	A	S	T	E
L	O	P	E		R	E	G	I	S	T	E	R
O	W	E	S		U	S	O		E	L	L	A
P	A	W	S		M	T	V		L	O	L	L

82

T	O	Y		B	O	M	B		D	E	A	L
W	O	O		O	M	A	R		W	A	N	E
E	D	G	E	W	I	S	E		E	G	G	Y
E	L	U	L		T	H	R	I	L	L	E	D
D	E	R	M	A			S	T	E	L	E	
S	S	T		D	E	C	O	R		T	A	N
			A	T	R	I	A					
O	R	E		G	A	Y	L	E		L	A	M
D	O	N	D	I			L	H	A	S	A	
D	O	G	O	O	D	E	R		E	S	P	Y
E	M	I	T		I	R	O	N	W	E	E	D
S	E	N	T		P	I	T	A		R	C	A
T	R	E	Y		S	E	A	N		S	T	Y

83

I	R	A	Q		E	P	O	S		F	R	Y
D	U	D	E		M	A	N	Y		R	I	O
E	G	A	D		I	C	O	N		E	N	G
A	S	P		I	R	K		O	M	E	G	A
			T	I	N		E	D	D	Y		
P	R	I	O	R	I	T	Y		R	A	T	E
R	E	N	D	E	R		E	L	I	N	O	R
Y	O	G	I		M	E	D	I	A	T	O	R
		N	E	A	T		A	D	E			
H	A	R	E	M		C	U	R		R	A	H
O	W	E		B	A	H	S		P	O	G	O
P	O	E		E	P	E	E		T	O	N	E
E	L	K		R	O	D	S		A	M	I	D

84

K	I	W	I		F	U	R		W	A	T	T
A	V	O	N		I	K	E		A	C	H	E
N	A	R	D		S	E	W		D	E	E	R
E	N	M	E	S	H		A	R	I	S	E	N
			E	E	Y	O	R	E				
W	A	N	D	A		A	D	S		A	R	C
A	V	A		L	A	S	S	O		P	E	A
F	E	E		A	N	I		L	A	T	E	R
			N	A	S	S	E	R				
A	B	B	O	T	T		I	S	L	A	N	D
G	R	A	B		O	W	N		E	V	E	R
R	U	S	E		M	O	E		N	A	S	A
A	T	T	Y		Y	E	W		E	R	S	T

85

P	H	R	A	S	E		G	A	L	A	S
L	O	O	T	E	D		B	E	R	I	N	G
A	B	A	T	E	D		O	R	I	E	N	T
N	O	N	E	T		D	O	M	E			
			S	H	E	I	K		L	A	R	D
P	R	O	T	E	G	E			H	O	E
A	I	R	S		O	H	M		V	A	I	N
L	T	D			A	U	D	I	B	L	Y
L	A	O	S		A	R	G	O	T			
			H	I	N	D		N	A	B	O	B
R	O	C	O	C	O		L	A	M	O	U	R
P	R	O	V	E	N		O	T	I	O	S	E
M	O	W	E	D			T	E	N	T	E	D

86

N	I	F	T	Y		B	E	R	A	T	E
A	R	U	B	A		C	A	L	I	P	E	R
B	A	N	A	L		R	A	I	N	I	N	G
			U	T	E		D	A	D	O
T	A	L	C		E	A	S	E			
O	G	E	E		E	K	E	D		P	B	S
R	E	F	O	R	M		M	O	S	A	I	C
N	E	T		H	E	E	P		A	T	T	U
			O	D	O	R		G	E	E	D
F	A	D	O			S	E	A			
I	S	R	A	E	L	I		L	E	A	S	H
S	T	E	T	S	O	N		L	A	U	R	A
T	I	G	H	T	S		Y	U	K	O	N

87

R	O	O	F		B	A	R		A	D	D	S
O	N	T	O		O	P	E		C	H	A	T
M	E	I	R		B	O	P		I	O	T	A
E	R	S	E		B	R	O	A	D	W	A	Y
			T	S	E	T	S	E			
S	H	R	E	W	D		E	N	R	I	C	O
A	M	B	L	E				E	E	L	E	R
C	O	I	L	E	D		P	A	L	L	E	T
			T	E	R	E	S	A			
G	L	A	S	S	F	U	L		T	U	F	T
A	I	N	U		E	B	O		I	S	L	E
G	R	A	D		A	L	T		O	M	E	N
E	A	T	S		T	E	A		N	A	E	S

88

D	A	S	H	E	D		V	E	N	A	L
O	R	N	E	R	Y		P	I	L	A	T	E
R	E	O	P	E	N		L	E	M	M	O	N
Y	A	W		B	A	S	I	N		E	N	S
			S	U	S	P	E	N	D		
T	R	I	E	S	T	E		A	E	G	I	S
N	O	D	E		Y	A	K		P	A	R	A
T	E	A	M	S		K	E	S	T	R	E	L
			S	T	R	E	T	C	H		
A	W	E		E	A	R	T	H		S	I	C
S	H	R	I	E	K		L	E	G	A	T	O
P	O	O	D	L	E		E	M	O	T	E	D
S	A	S	S	Y		S	E	V	E	R	E

89

F	I	N	N		P	R	O		B	L	O	T
A	S	I	A		E	O	N		R	I	S	E
L	E	N	I	E	N	C	E		A	B	L	E
L	E	A	F	Y					I	R	O	N
			E	T	A	M	I	N	E			
R	E	M		L	I	L	A	C		T	E	T
A	M	A		A	B	I	D	E		T	K	O
P	U	P		S	I	S	A	L		O	E	R
		M	A	H	A	T	M	A				
S	W	A	N					N	A	I	V	E
H	I	K	E		W	I	L	D	W	O	O	D
A	L	E	A		P	O	E		E	N	I	D
H	E	R	R		M	U	D		D	A	D	A

90

S	L	O	G	A	N			I	D	A	H	O
T	I	R	A	D	E		M	O	A	N	E	D
O	P	E	N	E	R		E	N	C	O	R	E
P	S	S	T		V	C	R		T	A	B	S
			R	O	Y	A	L	T	Y			
S	A	T	Y	R		N	I	B	L	I	C	K
P	T	A		I	R	A	N	I		C	U	E
A	M	O	R	O	U	S		L	E	E	R	Y
			I	N	S	T	A	L	L			
D	E	E	P		T	A	U		E	D	E	N
A	L	L	E	G	E		D	E	V	I	S	E
M	A	S	S	E	D		E	V	E	R	T	S
E	N	A	T	E			N	A	N	T	E	S

91

T	H	E	Y		E	W	E		H	O	S	T
B	A	L	I		G	A	S		O	B	O	E
S	L	U	E		O	T	T		A	I	D	A
P	O	L	L		I	C	E	C	R	E	A	M
			D	A	S	H	E	R				
S	C	H	I	S	M		M	A	S	S	E	S
O	P	E	N	S				Y	O	U	T	H
B	A	N	G	O	R		B	O	M	B	A	Y
			R	E	F	I	N	E				
C	R	Y	S	T	A	L	S		W	I	P	E
H	O	O	P		P	A	T		H	A	U	L
I	L	K	A		E	R	R		A	G	N	I
N	E	O	N		R	E	O		T	O	Y	S

92

I	S	L	E	T			A	S	S	I	G	N
O	P	E	N	E	D		S	T	E	R	E	O
W	A	N	D	E	R		H	U	M	A	N	E
A	R	T	E	M	I	S		P	I	N	T	S
			A	S	P	I	R	E				
B	E	A	R		R	A	F		M	B	A	
A	B	C		E	B	O	N	Y		T	E	N
A	B	E		T	I	C		E	V	E	N	
			E	T	C	H	E	S				
M	A	K	E	R			O	U	R	S	E	L	F
A	L	U	M	N	A		G	R	E	T	E	L
A	E	R	I	A	L		S	E	N	A	T	E
M	E	T	T	L	E			D	E	L	T	A

93

```
R E P O _ H A D _ S P I N
O L A V _ E V E _ A L G A
M A R E _ D A P _ R U N S
A T O N E D _ O S I R I S
N E D _ L A P S E _ A T E
_ D Y E D _ L I T T L E R
_ _ R E G A T T A _ _
U T T E R L Y _ L I R A _
R A H _ L E A V E _ E L I
B Y E B Y E _ A D R I F T
A L S O _ F O P _ I N R E
N O E L _ U R I _ T E E M
E R S T _ L T D _ A D D S
```

94

```
D R A M A S _ _ B E A R S
A T H O M E _ W A M P U M
L E A D E D _ I M B I B E
_ E N A C T _ R A Y E
B E S S _ T A S T Y _ _
R A T T L E R _ A O R T A
A R E _ A D D A X _ A W N
E L M A N _ O P I N I O N
_ _ L I S Z T _ E L S E
O R A L _ T O N G A _ _
M E D U S A _ E N T A I L
E N E R G Y _ S A L I V A
N O N E T _ _ S T Y L E D
```

95

```
A R E N A S _ P R E E N S
I N S E C T _ R E G R E T
D A P P E R _ A P O L L O
_ _ A D A G I O _ E L L
S E A L _ P O S S E _ _
E L D _ _ N E E D F U L
A M A H _ E D D _ O L G A
M O M E N T O _ _ E L K
_ _ P E A L E _ E D I E
T A N _ A M A N D A _ _
A G O U T I _ T O R P I D
L I S T E N _ E L T O R O
C O H E R E _ R E H E A T
```

96

```
J A C K _ M E M O _ E K E
I D L E _ A X E L _ D E N
G R E Y _ J A D E _ G E T
G I N _ R O M _ O P I N E
L A C I E R _ _ L E A R
E N H A N C E _ E A R N S
_ _ M E A N E S T _ _
P L E B E _ G E S T A L T
R A N I _ _ R E E V E S
E R E C T _ D I N _ A V E
S I S _ E T R E _ B L A T
T A C _ M A Y S _ E O N S
O T O _ P O S T _ A N T E
```

97

F	E	Y		I	S	N	T		A	S	T	A
R	A	E		S	C	A	B		L	I	E	N
E	R	A		L	A	N	A		D	E	N	T
U	N	R	E	E	L		F	O	R	T	H	
D	E	L	E		P	O	S	E		R	E	E
	D	Y	N	E		K	I	T		A	R	M
			T	R	A	C	E					
U	S	N		H	O	P		D	O	R	A	
N	E	E		A	D	I	T		T	A	U	T
E	A	T	E	N		A	T	T	I	R	E	
A	R	T	S		R	O	U	E		N	O	R
S	E	E	P		Y	A	P	S		E	R	R
E	D	D	Y		E	K	E	S		D	A	Y

98

N	E	G	E	V			A	R	I	S	E
I	R	O	N	E	D		E	L	E	V	E	N
K	R	A	M	E	R		W	I	Z	A	R	D
E	S	T	E		I	R	E		O	N	E	S
		S	A	V	A	R	I	N				
C	A	S	H	I	E	R		N	E	A	T	H
O	D	E		D	R	E	A	D		M	O	A
O	S	A	G	E		B	R	I	S	T	O	L
		A	D	M	I	R	A	L			
A	V	I	S		E	T	A		O	K	R	A
S	O	C	K	E	T		Y	A	W	N	E	D
S	T	E	E	L	E		S	L	E	E	V	E
T	E	S	T	Y			T	R	E	S	S

99

S	C	R	E	A	M		F	R	E	E	D
T	R	E	N	D	Y		C	L	U	B	B	Y
L	E	A	S	E	S		H	O	M	B	R	E
O	W	L		S	T	A	I	R		S	O	D
			S	T	E	N	C	I	L			
C	O	N	C	E	R	T		D	A	U	B	S
O	L	I	O		Y	I	P		D	R	I	P
B	E	B	O	P		Q	U	A	L	I	T	Y
		T	R	O	U	N	C	E			
E	R	E		O	M	E	G	A		G	N	P
G	O	D	I	V	A		E	C	L	A	I	R
G	U	N	N	E	R		N	I	E	L	L	O
S	T	A	N	D			T	A	I	L	E	D

100

I	N	C	A		T	O	T		S	W	A	P
D	U	A	L		A	N	A		E	A	R	L
E	T	N	A		S	O	B		E	L	L	A
A	R	A	R	A	T		O	A	K	L	E	Y
L	I	L		V	I	S	O	R		O	N	E
	A	S	L	E	E	P		T	A	P	E	D
		E	R	R	A	T	I	C				
S	H	E	E	R		T	E	S	T	E	R	
I	O	N		E	L	E	N	A		N	E	T
F	A	C	A	D	E		A	N	D	R	E	W
T	R	I	P		A	N	N		E	A	S	E
E	S	N	E		S	A	C		A	G	E	E
R	E	A	R		H	E	Y		R	E	S	T

101

P	A	C	E	R				C	R	A	C	K
I	R	O	N	E	R		O	N	E	I	L	L
N	E	A	R	B	Y		U	N	T	R	U	E
T	A	X	I		A	F	T		I	S	E	E
			C	O	N	I	F	E	R			
A	L	L	O	W		N	I	N	E	V	E	H
R	E	O		N	O	L	T	E		I	O	U
F	O	N	S	E	C	A		R	O	A	S	T
			T	R	E	N	T	O	N			
A	C	R	E		A	D	E		I	B	I	D
L	A	U	R	E	N		S	T	O	O	G	E
O	B	S	E	S	S		T	E	N	D	O	N
E	S	T	O	P				D	Y	E	R	S

102

O	T	T	O		F	O	B		T	I	C	S
L	O	O	P		A	L	L		A	N	A	T
E	R	S	T		T	E	A		U	L	N	A
I	R	S		R	E	S	T	S		A	O	K
N	I	E	C	E	S		A	W	H	I	L	E
	D	D	A	Y		O	N	E	I	D	A	
			S	N	O	R	T	E	D			
	O	C	T	A	V	E		T	E	E	M	
A	D	H	E	R	E		S	E	S	T	E	T
L	E	A		D	R	A	I	N		U	T	E
O	S	L	O		A	L	F		A	D	E	N
U	S	E	D		G	U	T		M	E	R	E
D	A	T	A		E	M	S		P	S	S	T

103

R	I	A	N	T				H	O	N	E	S
I	N	D	I	A	N		E	E	Y	O	R	E
F	R	I	N	G	E		U	P	S	A	L	A
F	E	T	E		E	A	R		T	H	E	M
			T	A	D	P	O	L	E			
P	O	L	Y	M	E	R		E	R	A	T	O
B	A	Y		E	D	I	T	H		R	B	I
S	K	E	I	N		C	O	A	S	T	A	L
			A	D	J	O	U	R	N			
S	C	A	M		E	T	C		I	M	A	M
T	R	I	B	A	L		A	T	T	I	R	E
A	E	R	I	A	L		N	I	C	K	E	L
B	E	E	C	H				C	H	E	S	T

104

E	G	G		K	N	O	W		B	A	T	T
S	O	L		N	O	R	A		E	T	R	E
C	O	O		I	R	O	N		S	T	A	R
A	B	B	O	T	T		T	O	T	A	L	S
P	E	E	N		H	A	I	G		C	E	E
E	R	S	E			S	N	E	A	K	E	R
			A	V	E	N	G	E	R			
V	I	L	L	A	G	E		T	A	N	S	
I	D	A		L	O	R	I		E	N	O	W
R	E	N	N	E	T		R	E	L	I	V	E
T	A	C	O		I	N	K	Y		M	I	D
U	T	E	S		S	E	E	R		A	C	E
E	E	R	Y		M	O	D	E		L	E	N

105

A	F	T	O	N		M	O	R	O	S	E
P	E	O	R	I	A		A	R	E	T	H	A
T	E	R	C	E	T		P	O	T	T	E	R
		M	A	C	A	W			R	O	M	P
A	W	E		E	L	A	P	S	E			
V	A	N	S		A	D	O	R	N	I	N	G
A	C	T	I	O	N		S	O	C	C	E	R
R	O	S	S	E	T	T	I		H	E	R	A
			T	R	A	I	T	S		C	O	B
F	U	M	E			S	I	T	A	R		
U	S	U	R	P	S		V	O	T	E	R	S
E	M	I	L	I	O		E	N	T	A	I	L
L	A	R	Y	N	X		Y	U	M	M	Y	

106

A	D	E	S	T	E		G	Y	R	A	T	E
B	A	T	H	E	S		R	E	E	S	E	S
B	R	U	I	N	S		I	N	S	E	R	T
R	E	I	N		E	S	P		C	A	N	E
			T	O	N	N	E	A	U			
M	A	J	O	R	C	A		L	E	D	G	E
A	G	O		S	E	P	A	L		E	A	R
R	E	T	R	O		P	L	I	A	B	L	E
		I	N	T	E	G	E	R				
B	A	R	B		O	D	E		R	O	T	E
I	S	O	B	A	R		R	A	I	D	E	R
A	S	S	O	R	T		I	R	V	I	N	G
S	T	A	N	C	E		A	M	E	N	D	S

107

O	G	R	E		U	R	I		T	W	I	G
B	A	I	L		P	E	N		R	A	R	E
I	N	C	A		S	O	D		O	R	A	L
E	T	H	N	I	C		Y	E	W			
			D	R	A	W		X	E	R	I	C
F	A	L	S	E	L	Y		C	L	A	R	A
E	G	O		L	E	A	V	E		K	O	S
L	I	A	N	A		T	O	R	R	E	N	T
L	O	D	E	N		T	Y	P	O			
			A	D	E		A	T	T	U	N	E
B	R	E	R		V	E	G		A	R	I	L
Y	E	L	L		I	V	E		T	A	N	K
E	E	L	Y		L	A	D		E	N	O	S

108

B	O	W		E	T	O	N		E	A	S	E
O	R	E		L	E	V	I		D	I	A	L
L	E	E		F	R	E	T		E	D	G	Y
A	L	D	O		E	R	W	I	N			
			A	U	S	T	I	N		O	U	R
S	I	E	R	R	A		T	S	E	T	S	E
A	C	R	E	S				U	R	I	E	L
N	O	R	D	I	C		B	R	A	S	S	Y
E	N	S		N	O	B	L	E	S			
			Z	E	B	R	A		E	W	E	R
A	N	T	E		R	A	Z	E		A	P	O
M	E	I	R		A	V	O	N		R	E	B
P	O	C	O		S	A	N	G		D	E	E

109

R	I	A	L		D	A	N		D	R	A	M
O	L	L	A		I	K	E		I	O	N	A
S	K	I	P		A	A	H		P	U	T	T
E	A	T	I	N	G		R	I	P	E	S	T
			N	U	R	T	U	R	E			
L	I	E		M	A	E		I	R	A	T	E
E	O	S		E	M	E	N	D		S	I	R
T	U	T	O	R		T	A	I		H	E	R
			W	A	S	H	T	U	B			
A	P	O	L	L	O		U	M	L	A	U	T
L	O	N	I		N	O	R		E	S	P	Y
A	L	E	S		E	T	A		S	T	O	P
N	O	S	H		S	O	L		S	I	N	E

110

D	O	T	E		C	O	K	E		C	A	P
A	N	I	L		E	L	U	L		A	L	L
R	E	P	S		O	D	D	S		R	T	E
K	I	T	E	D			Z	A	G	R	E	B
E	D	O		E	S	A	U		E	I	R	E
N	A	P		P	E	P		A	M	E	S	
			O	A	S	I	S					
	B	A	R	T		E	O	N		C	U	R
A	R	L	O		E	S	N	E		A	R	E
G	U	I	T	A	R			R	A	J	A	H
A	T	E		B	R	A	Y		C	O	N	E
P	U	N		B	O	N	O		E	L	I	A
E	S	S		E	L	A	N		S	E	C	T

111

E	P	E	E	S		A	G	R	E	E	D
E	R	A	S	E	S		T	R	E	B	L	E
R	O	T	T	E	N		M	A	D	A	M	E
Y	A	S	H	M	A	K		S	E	N	O	R
			E	S	P	O	U	S	E			
C	H	A	R		R	H	O	M	B	U	S	
P	A	L		R	E	F		E	M	U		
A	N	T	I	G	U	A		L	A	P	P	
			P	E	N	N	A	M	E			
L	U	M	E	N		S	M	E	A	R	E	D
E	L	E	C	T	S		O	D	D	I	T	Y
A	N	N	A	L	S		K	E	E	N	A	N
F	A	U	C	E	T		A	N	K	L	E	

112

T	E	N	N		O	F	F		S	T	A	G
A	L	O	E		P	R	O		E	A	R	L
R	I	T	A		E	A	R		A	I	D	A
E	D	I	T	O	R		M	I	L	L	E	D
S	E	C		B	A	C	O	N		O	N	E
	D	E	A	L		A	S	S	O	R	T	S
			M	I	G	R	A	T	E			
U	P	R	I	G	H	T		A	R	I	A	
N	E	E		E	A	S	E	L		O	R	O
T	R	E	N	D	S		G	L	I	D	E	D
O	S	L	O		T	H	Y		M	I	N	E
L	I	E	D		L	O	P		A	N	A	T
D	A	D	E		Y	E	T		M	E	S	S

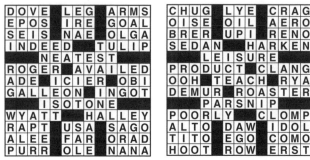

113

```
D O V E   L E G   A R M S
E P O S   I R E   G O A L
S E I S   N A E   O L G A
I N D E E D     T U L I P
      N E A T E S T
R O G E R   A V A I L E D
A D E   I C I E R   O B I
G A L L E O N   I N G O T
      I S O T O N E
W Y A T T     H A L L E Y
R A P T   U S A   S A G O
A L E E   F A R   O R A D
P U R R   O L E   N A N A
```

114

```
C H U G   L Y E   C R A G
O I S E   O I L   A E R O
B R E R   U P I   R E N O
S E D A N   H A R K E N
      L E I S U R E
P R O D U C T   C L A N G
O O H   T E A C H   R Y A
D E M U R   R O A S T E R
      P A R S N I P
P O O R L Y     C L O M P
A L T O   D A W   I D O L
T I T O   E G O   C O M O
H O O T   R O W   E R S T
```

115

```
O W N   E Z R A   R U S S
A H A   S E E M   O N T O
T A T   T B S P   A L A R
E L U D E R     A D O P T
N E R O   A S P S   A L I
  R E T E   T O W   D E E
      M A R I A
P S I   E L I   N A I F
E T C   R E P O   B R E D
R E E D Y     D E C O D E
S E M I   L A D D   N O B
O L A V   E K E D   I R A
N E N E   N A R Y   C A R
```

116

```
S P C A   F E Z   U T A H
H E A R T I L Y   M I M E
Y A M M E R E D   B R A M
      T I M E   R E T S
I T S     N I C H E
T Y P I N G   O O L O N G
C R U D E     B L U E R
H E R O I C   C O A R S E
      L L A M A   S T Y
S A R A   E A R P
A L O T   S P R O U T E D
F A I R   A L I E N A T E
E E L Y   R E E   O M A N
```

117

P	A	I	R		B	O	G		M	A	T	E
A	G	N	I		E	R	R		O	N	E	R
L	E	N	O		T	S	A	R	I	N	A	S
E	D	O		P	R	O	S	E		E	R	E
		C	L	E	A	N	S	E	R			
T	R	E	A	T	Y		O	D	E	S	S	A
S	E	N	T					A	H	E	M	
P	O	T	I	O	N		A	F	L	O	A	T
		N	O	O	N	T	I	M	E			
E	L	K		P	R	I	O	R		H	U	N
B	O	N	D	S	M	E	N		L	O	S	E
A	G	I	O		A	C	E		E	R	M	A
N	O	T	E		L	E	D		S	N	A	P

118

S	K	E	I	N		G	L	A	N	C	E
K	I	T	T	E	N		L	A	R	I	A	T
I	N	N	A	T	E		U	G	A	N	D	A
D	E	A	L		V	A	T		R	E	E	L
			I	C	E	D	T	E	A			
S	E	C	C	O		V	O	L	T	A	G	E
A	A	H		S	T	I	N	T		V	A	N
W	R	E	A	T	H	S		O	P	A	L	S
		C	A	R	E	E	N	S				
L	I	S	T		O	D	D		Y	A	R	E
O	N	E	I	D	A		D	E	C	L	A	W
C	R	A	V	A	T		A	D	H	E	R	E
H	E	R	E	B	Y			D	E	F	E	R

119

I	V	E	S		C	L	E	F		L	O	S
V	I	S	A		L	E	V	I		O	W	L
Y	E	T	I		O	V	E	N		L	E	O
			L	I	V	E	R		T	A	N	G
H	I	E		S	E	E	T	H	E			
I	N	C	H	O	N		S	E	S	T	E	T
S	C	R	U	B				A	L	I	K	E
S	A	U	N	A	S		E	V	A	D	E	D
			C	R	E	A	T	E		E	S	S
S	I	G	H		A	M	U	S	E			
T	O	O		A	V	I	D		X	R	A	Y
E	W	E		G	E	N	E		A	N	N	A
W	A	S		E	R	O	S		M	A	A	M

120

A	B	A	S	E		A	N	G	E	L	A
D	E	S	I	G	N		D	E	A	L	E	R
D	E	P	L	O	Y		Z	O	Y	S	I	A
			E	S	P			L	E	S	S	
O	M	E	N		D	O	U	S	E			
P	A	Y	T	V		I	K	E		M	R	S
A	D	E		E	E	L	E	R		E	E	K
H	E	R		A	R	E		B	U	N	N	Y
			S	L	A	D	E		L	U	T	E
A	S	T	A			N	O	T				
F	L	A	V	O	R		I	R	I	S	E	S
A	U	R	O	R	A		D	A	M	A	G	E
R	E	A	R	E	D			L	O	D	G	E

121

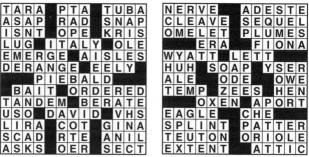

E	A	R	F	U	L		F	E	R	A	L
A	V	E	R	S	E		A	L	L	U	R	E
V	I	S	I	O	N		N	O	T	I	N	G
E	S	T	E		T	S	K		O	N	E	S
			N	E	I	T	H	E	R			
T	W	I	D	D	L	E		N	O	R	T	H
O	A	R		I	S	L	E	S		A	H	A
T	R	A	I	L		L	A	U	G	H	E	D
			D	E	B	A	S	E	R			
R	I	P	E		U	R	I		A	G	I	N
E	C	L	A	I	R		E	L	P	A	S	O
T	E	U	T	O	N		S	I	P	P	E	D
E	S	S	E	N		T	E	A	S	E	S	

122

G	I	V	E	R		B	O	O		S	I	B
U	R	I	A	H		O	U	T	L	I	N	E
T	E	A	S	E		L	I	T	U	R	G	Y
			T	A	M	E		G	E	E	S	
T	E	R	M		A	R	C	S				
A	P	I	A		G	O	A	L		J	O	T
L	E	N	N	O	N		S	Y	R	U	P	Y
L	E	G		N	E	N	E		U	R	A	N
			E	T	U	I		P	Y	L	E	
S	C	A	R		G	N	A	T				
N	O	S	E	B	A	G		S	U	G	A	R
U	P	S	C	A	L	E		I	R	E	N	E
G	E	T		A	P	T		F	E	L	I	X

123

T	A	R	A		P	T	A		T	U	B	A
A	S	A	P		R	A	D		S	N	A	P
I	S	N	T		O	P	E		K	R	I	S
L	U	G		I	T	A	L	Y		O	L	E
E	M	E	R	G	E		A	I	S	L	E	S
D	E	R	A	N	G	E		E	E	L	Y	
			P	I	E	B	A	L	D			
	B	A	I	T		O	R	D	E	R	E	D
T	A	N	D	E	M		B	E	R	A	T	E
U	S	O		D	A	V	I	D		V	H	S
L	I	R	A		C	O	T		G	I	N	A
S	C	A	D		R	T	E		A	N	I	L
A	S	K	S		O	E	R		S	E	C	T

124

N	E	R	V	E		A	D	E	S	T	E
C	L	E	A	V	E		S	E	Q	U	E	L
O	M	E	L	E	T		P	L	U	M	E	S
			E	R	A		F	I	O	N	A	
W	Y	A	T	T		L	E	T	T			
H	U	H		S	O	A	P		Y	S	E	R
A	L	E		O	D	E		O	W	E		
T	E	M	P		Z	E	E	S		H	E	N
			O	X	E	N		A	P	O	R	T
E	A	G	L	E		C	H	E				
S	P	L	I	N	T		P	A	T	T	E	R
T	E	U	T	O	N		O	R	I	O	L	E
E	X	T	E	N	T		A	T	T	I	C	

125

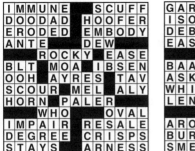

I	M	M	U	N	E			S	C	U	F	F
D	O	O	D	A	D		H	O	O	F	E	R
E	R	O	D	E	D		E	M	B	O	D	Y
A	N	T	E			D	E	W				
			R	O	C	K	Y		E	A	S	E
B	L	T		M	O	A		I	B	S	E	N
O	O	H		A	Y	R	E	S		T	A	V
S	C	O	U	R		M	E	L		A	L	Y
H	O	R	N		P	A	L	E	R			
			W	H	O			O	V	A	L	
I	M	P	A	I	R		R	E	S	A	L	E
D	E	G	R	E	E		C	R	I	S	P	S
S	T	A	Y	S			A	R	N	E	S	S

126

G	A	R	A	G	E			D	A	M	E	S
I	S	O	B	A	R		F	I	N	A	L	E
D	E	B	A	T	E		A	R	G	Y	L	E
E	A	S	T			U	K	E				
		E	R	W	I	N		L	A	N	I	
B	A	A		E	O	N		I	S	L	E	T
A	S	K		S	K	E	E	T		E	W	E
W	H	I	S	T		R	A	E		A	T	M
L	E	N	A		U	T	U	R	N			
		M	A	R			Y	A	R	E		
A	R	O	U	N	D		S	U	L	L	E	N
B	U	R	E	A	U		P	R	O	V	E	D
S	M	E	L	T			A	N	N	A	L	S

127

M	O	R	K		G	A	M		I	B	A	R
O	V	E	N		O	N	E		O	L	L	A
N	I	N	O		O	D	D		D	U	E	T
A	D	D	L	E	D		A	P	I	E	C	E
		L	A	B	E	L	E	D				
E	N	G		R	Y	A		R	E	A	R	M
S	O	N		N	E	G	E	V		A	H	A
P	R	U	N	E		E	V	A		H	O	P
		A	S	T	R	I	D	E				
D	I	L	U	T	E		D	E	R	A	I	L
A	G	O	G		R	O	E		R	I	V	E
M	O	T	H		R	A	N		O	R	A	N
E	R	S	T		A	R	T		R	E	N	O

128

P	A	D	S		S	I	B		R	O	T	A
U	T	A	H		L	O	U		E	P	I	C
N	E	N	E		O	U	R		C	U	R	E
			A	W	E		R	A	I	S	E	D
S	A	L	V	E		W	I	S	P			
C	R	U	E	T		O	T	H	E	L	L	O
A	N	N		T	A	R	O	T		I	A	N
R	E	A	D	E	R	S		R	E	E	V	E
			A	S	S	T		A	L	D	E	R
C	H	A	S	T	E		D	Y	E			
H	A	T	H		N	B	A		V	A	S	T
A	L	O	E		A	I	M		E	D	I	E
T	E	N	D		L	O	P		N	E	X	T

129

L	I	M	B	S			T	O	P	P	L	E
A	G	O	U	T	I		I	B	E	R	I	A
R	U	N	N	E	R		M	I	N	I	N	G
G	A	D		V	E	E		C	O	A	L	
E	N	A	M	E	L	S		V	E	R	G	E
R	A	Y	E		A	S	T	I		Y	E	T
			G	E	N	E	R	A	L			
A	C	T		E	D	N	A		E	D	G	E
S	H	I	R	K		C	I	S	T	E	R	N
S	A	N	E		E	L	Y		V	A	T	
E	N	G	A	G	E		E	N	C	O	D	E
S	E	L	D	O	M		R	O	U	T	E	R
S	L	E	E	T	S			D	E	E	D	S

130

D	O	W	S	E	S			R	A	B	A	T
A	B	R	A	D	E		C	E	R	I	S	E
D	I	E	T	E	R		I	A	M	B	I	C
E	E	N		N	A	S	A	L		B	A	H
			D	I	P	L	O	M	A			
P	A	N	A	C	E	A		B	O	S	S	
O	M	A	N		S	T	Y		E	R	I	K
P	A	G	E		H	I	S	T	O	R	Y	
			S	T	R	E	E	T	S			
R	N	A		E	A	R	L	E		R	E	D
O	O	L	O	N	G		D	A	M	O	N	E
M	E	D	U	S	A		E	D	I	S	O	N
E	L	A	T	E			D	Y	N	A	S	T

131

S	T	E	E	D	S		O	P	P	O	S	E
T	U	R	R	E	T		P	E	O	R	I	A
O	N	I	O	N	Y		I	N	T	E	N	T
L	A	N	D		L	O	N		A	S	K	S
			E	M	I	N	E	N	T			
K	I	N	D	E	S	T		I	O	W	A	N
I	R	A		E	T	A	P	E		I	V	E
P	E	N	D	S		R	E	C	I	T	E	D
			R	E	T	I	R	E	D			
S	A	G	A		R	O	C		E	U	R	O
T	R	I	P	L	E		E	R	A	S	E	R
E	I	L	E	E	N		N	A	T	A	N	T
P	A	D	D	E	D		T	H	E	F	T	S

132

H	O	M	E		G	E	L	S		A	P	O
A	D	E	N		E	R	A	S		B	E	G
M	E	L	D		N	E	W	T		E	R	R
			S	P	I	C	Y		S	L	U	E
P	H	I		L	A	T	E	N	T			
R	A	S	C	A	L		R	E	A	G	A	N
O	R	L	O	N				A	L	O	N	E
S	T	E	R	E	O		A	R	L	E	N	E
			A	D	M	I	R	E		S	A	D
T	E	L	L		E	N	T	R	Y			
O	L	E		A	L	E	E		O	N	C	E
G	A	T		K	E	R	R		H	I	E	D
A	M	T		A	T	T	Y		O	L	E	O

133

J	U	L	Y		F	C	C		G	L	O	P
E	R	I	E		O	O	H		E	I	R	E
F	A	L	A		O	D	A		L	E	A	S
F	L	A	R	E	D		P	S	E	U	D	O
			L	A	S	A	L	L	E			
S	A	T	Y	R		V	I	E		I	N	K
G	N	U		P	H	O	N	E		L	E	I
T	A	X		L	O	W		P	O	L	E	D
			P	U	R	S	U	E	D			
M	A	L	A	G	A		P	R	E	A	M	P
A	C	E	S		T	H	E		S	L	U	R
A	R	A	S		I	O	N		S	A	S	E
M	E	D	E		O	D	D		A	R	T	Y

134

E	V	I	L		A	S	H	E		D	N	A
M	A	N	E		D	A	U	B		A	I	R
O	L	D	S		S	C	H	O	O	N	E	R
T	I	E	S				H	U	L	A		
E	S	N	E		A	S	S	E	M	B	L	Y
	E	T	E	R	N	I	T	Y		E	O	S
			A	N	E	A	R					
P	E	A		G	I	N	G	E	R	L	Y	
O	V	E	R	S	E	A	S		A	L	O	T
N	E	R	O				M	A	D	E		
G	L	I	M	P	S	E	D		A	M	E	N
E	Y	E		S	A	R	A		D	A	L	E
E	N	S		I	M	A	M		A	S	S	T

135

A	M	A	T		C	A	P	T		A	N	T
L	A	N	I		A	R	E	A		I	O	U
E	R	I	C		B	R	A	D		N	O	R
			K	R	A	A	L		S	U	N	K
S	P	A		I	N	S	E	R	T			
C	A	N	A	D	A		D	I	R	E	C	T
A	L	I	B	I				T	A	B	L	E
B	E	L	O	N	G		A	U	P	A	I	R
			U	G	A	N	D	A		N	O	M
L	I	S	T		M	E	R	L	E			
A	O	K		M	I	S	O		N	E	V	E
W	W	I		A	N	T	I		O	L	A	V
N	A	P		P	E	S	T		W	I	N	E

136

O	P	E	C		R	I	O		O	R	C	A
W	O	V	E		E	L	M		N	U	L	L
E	K	E	D		S	K	I		E	N	O	L
D	Y	N	A	S	T		T	W	I	G	G	Y
			R	E	F	U	S	A	L			
B	L	T		S	U	N		C	L	E	R	K
B	O	B		S	L	I	C	K		F	Y	I
Q	U	A	S	I		T	A	I		T	A	T
			P	O	L	Y	M	E	R			
F	E	L	I	N	E		E	R	A	S	E	D
A	G	O	G		A	W	L		B	O	L	O
T	A	C	O		R	H	O		A	L	S	O
S	N	I	T		N	O	T		T	E	A	M

137

138

139